WHAT THEY DON'T TELL YOU

WHAT THEY DON'T TELL YOU
A SURVIVOR'S GUIDE TO BIBLICAL STUDIES

Michael Joseph Brown

WESTMINSTER
JOHN KNOX PRESS
LOUISVILLE · KENTUCKY

Scripture quotations from the New Revised Standard Version of the Bible are copyright © 1989 by the Division of Christian Education of the National Council of the Churches of Christ in the U.S.A. and are used by permission.

Cover photography by John Fitzgerald

First edition
Published by Westminster John Knox Press
Louisville, Kentucky

This book is printed on acid-free paper that meets the American National Standards Institute Z39.48 standard. ♾

PRINTED IN THE UNITED STATES OF AMERICA

04 05 06 07 08 09—10 9 8 7 6

Library of Congress Cataloging-in-Publication Data is on file at the Library of Congress, Washington, D.C.

ISBN 0-664-22220-X

To
Susan Wiltshire
and
Daniel Patte

Contents

Acknowledgments

Teaching is a grave and select responsibility. James 3:1 says, "Not many of you should become teachers, my brothers and sisters, for you know that we who teach will be judged with greater strictness." I have certainly found this to be true in my years of teaching. Coming into a classroom to teach can be an awesome experience, similar to coming into contact with the holy—that is, if the process is done properly. This book derives from my joys and sorrows in the classroom. It is the culmination of lectures, conversations, and debates carried out during my years at Wabash College in Crawfordsville, Indiana. In reality, if it had not been for my students at Wabash, this book would never have been written, for it was while I was there that I first learned the importance of student and teacher "speaking the same language."

Simply recognizing my students at Wabash is not sufficient to account for this book. Its real roots go all the way back to my senior ministry project when I was a student at the University of Chicago Divinity School. While at Chicago I served as assistant pastor for Greater Institutional African Methodist Episcopal Church. One of my duties was to teach the weekly Bible study class. While teaching that course I began to believe that scholarship could serve the interests of the average believer. The only problem, I realized, is that scholarship is wedded to technical language and theory in such a way as to repel many who might benefit from its insights. I began to try to find a way to overcome the limitations of scholarly language—to translate scholarship, if you will—so that my students could feel the empowerment I felt in reading the Bible with a critical eye. So my initial thanks must go to that original Bible study group, who persevered with me in planting the seeds for this project.

I would like to thank my students and colleagues at Wabash College, along with the people at Greater Institutional. I am especially indebted to William Placher, who read the initial drafts of this manuscript and made suggestions for its improvement. Bill has a knack for making the profound sound so simple, and I drew on his abilities in creating this work. I am indebted to all the students who took my courses at Wabash, but especially to a few whose conversations with me helped me target this book properly. Thanks to Zachary Scott May, Scott Snell, and Derek M. Dotson for sharing with me their insights into what went on in class. Special thanks to Joshua Patty for his intellectual acumen and his participation in my courses. I wish him well as he prepares to follow in my footsteps at the University of Chicago Divinity School. I do not think I would have ended my tenure at Wabash with such affection if it had not been for Kim L. King II. Kim's presence in class and on campus added to my experience in ways he will never know. The synchronicity that brought us together compels me to believe in the providential purposes of God. I do not think that I will ever again come across such a person as Kim, but if I do, I will certainly know that one's cup can run over with divine blessings. I would also like to thank Stephanie Egnotovich, my editor at Westminster John Knox Press, for her great editorial insights. Ultimately, this manuscript is readable because of her input. Finally, I would like to thank Raymond B. Williams and the Wabash Center for Teaching and Learning in Theology and Religion. The spark for this project occurred while I was visiting Israel on a grant from the Wabash Center. The design of the grant was to improve my teaching. Although this book was not the outcome I had in mind, I believe that this project has made me a better teacher. I just hope that my teaching continues to flourish, because teaching is important.

Prolegomena

Prolegomena. I love that word. Basically, it means all that "stuff" that has to be said before you get down to what it is you actually *want* to say. Biblical studies is rife with prolegomena. Although biblical scholars make the whole thing look easy, that is only because they have already absorbed all the necessary prolegomena. Unfortunately, sometimes those scholars are not forthcoming about all the prolegomena that make biblical studies successful. So, after spending many hours in class teaching my students the "rules" for interpreting texts—rules that I learned over the course of twelve years—I decided I should write down some of these rules of thumb for biblical studies so that students would have a handy guide available when they study the Bible.

I have tried to make this book as accessible as possible. In other words, I have done my best to avoid using pesky technical terms and lengthy historical explanations when laying out these rules of thumb. What I have done is to "translate" some foundational concepts in biblical studies into an idiom more people can understand.

My sole purpose is to make explicit the mind-set (or presuppositions) that scholars use implicitly when interpreting the Bible. So I also *try* to avoid discussing particular methods of exegesis, or interpretation. There are many different methods out in the academic marketplace, and there are also some very good handbooks that describe how each method works. Instead, I focus on the fundamental basis for interpreting biblical texts, the *historical-critical method.* This was actually an easy choice, because *all* biblical scholars, whether or not they still follow that method completely, have been trained in it. Moreover, it is the most frequently used method in classes introducing the New Testament or Hebrew Bible. (See the section entitled "Methods of Biblical Interpretation," below.)

This guide is divided into four chapters. In chapter 1, I clarify the difference between the aims of Bible study (mainly devotional) and the aims of biblical scholarship (i.e., science [German *Wissenschaft*]: systematic and critical study of a particular body of data according to the prevailing methods of the field). I also provide information about the basics of the Bible, guidance about how to prepare for academic biblical scholarship, a short note on the history of biblical scholarship, and an overview of methods of biblical interpretation.

In chapter 2 I lay down rules of thumb for reading and interpreting biblical texts. Of course, this list is not exhaustive, nor are the rules meant to be taken as hard and fast rules that can never be broken. That is why I call them "rules of thumb" instead of just "rules." Rules carry with them the weight of scholarly authority and the fruits of experience and tradition. That is, they are theoretical principles that govern previously agreed upon, general ways of arguing applied to a particular case. They are similar to the rules of procedure in trying court cases. Some of these rules, for example, about the extent of attorney-client privilege or the meaning of unlawful search and seizure, are open to various interpretations. I am not trying to establish any such grand principles. Quite the contrary, I am laying down some principles or methods of procedure based on experience and common sense.

In chapter 3 I help students sort through the variety of perspectives that make up the world of biblical scholarship. This is important because many people approach biblical studies as they would mathematics. That is, they believe that if you follow the method properly, only one "right" answer is possible. Without becoming overly theoretical, let me say that the process of biblical interpretation is not that easy, and it takes an astute reader to cross these waters without drowning.

Finally, in chapter 4 I deal with an issue scholars do not like to discuss: surviving what biblical scholarship does to you. We all come to the biblical text with some ideas about what it means. Biblical scholarship often causes us to question those ideas, and without some way to understand and integrate our experience and our *belief*, we run the risk that our encounter with the academic world of biblical scholarship will damage us rather than empower us.

I hope that this book will serve as an aid to learning and conducting academic biblical scholarship. It is not meant to be used as an introduction to the Bible. Rather, it is meant to be used in conjunction with texts dealing with the analysis of biblical literature. By discussing the implicit workings of biblical scholarship, I hope to demystify the discipline for those who are new to it. When you begin to understand the basis upon which Bible scholars make their judgments, you are empowered to participate fully in the ongoing creativity that is biblical scholarship. Without this information, you can become disenchanted with biblical scholars and their work, and thus miss some of the keen insights that make biblical scholarship an impressive and thoughtful discipline. What Bible scholars do is important to our understanding not only of particular religions, like those of the ancient Israelites or early Christians, but of what it means to be a human being in relationship with other human beings.

1

The Aims of Bible Study and the Aims of Biblical Scholarship

Why Biblical Scholarship Is Not Sunday School

It is the first thing I tell my students when they enter my classes: *the academic study of the Bible is not the same thing as the kind of study that is conducted in your Bible study or Sunday school.* Students often don't understand the importance of this statement until they try to write their first academic paper, and then it is almost too late. For until then, they don't understand that what goes on in biblical scholarship is different from what goes on in our faith communities. Although "the academy" often seeks to have a good relationship with the church, more often than not, each side ends up frustrated at the other's stubbornness. The problem is that the academy and the church operate under different sets of assumptions and with different mind-sets. (I am not saying that one view is right and the other is wrong. They are just different views, and they are different for very valid reasons.)

When I was a pastor, parishioners would get frustrated with me because I would not make grand and authoritative statements about what I believed was a superficial reading of the Bible, based on my training in biblical scholarship. Even more, as a scholar I refused to make the common jump my parishioners easily made when reading the Bible—the jump from reading a text to explaining its significance for their personal faith journeys. I had learned to be more cautious than that. One thing I have learned from the academic study of the Bible is that not everything the Bible talks about is relevant to my faith journey. For example, very little in the book of Leviticus is relevant to my life as a Christian in the twenty-first century. But many people in the pews feel that they *must* get something relevant from Leviticus because it is identified as the word of God, and so they do almost anything to construct a meaning for the text in order to justify the text's existence. I have seen such "faith gymnastics" in parishes all over the country.

Bible study as it is conducted in the average church too often has to do with what I call "self-help" religion. That is, many people come to Bible studies not to hear what the text is saying, but to reaffirm themselves and their faith perspective. Bible studies are often the Christian version of self-help groups like Alcoholics Anonymous. People gather together, read the big book, and share their personal trials and achievements with one another. *There is nothing wrong with this.* However, it is not what happens when you walk into a college classroom and begin the academic study of the Hebrew Bible or the New Testament. The aims of parish Bible study are devotional and geared toward personal improvement. These are very important goals for people aspiring to live productive religious lives, but they are not the goals of the academic study of scripture.

Some of the most impressive and faithful religious people I have ever known did not possess an academic understanding of scripture. They had an understanding of what it meant to be a thinking, acting, responsible person before God, and they lived according to that insight. They read the Bible from the perspective of a person seriously trying to live in the light of God's will. Remember, an academic understanding of the Bible is not necessary to be a good Christian. That is, while I sincerely feel that an academic understanding of the Bible can assist people in their faith journeys, scriptural acumen is no guarantee that living a properly Christian life will result. If knowledge of scripture—particularly academic knowledge—were necessary for salvation then only scholars would be true Christians or Jews, and this is certainly not the case. Biblical scholarship is not "church knowledge." In fact, modern biblical scholarship has little connection to church authority. While many biblical scholars are religious people, established religious institutions generally do not control what biblical scholars think, teach, and write.

One of the aims of academic biblical scholarship is to uncover and relay the means by which knowledge has been gathered and, if appropriate, identify the inadequacies of the scholarship. This is a far different perspective from the one that sees the Bible as containing doctrines and self-evident truths. According to scholars, biblical interpretation is defined simply as *the process of understanding, and possibly also explaining, what the Bible means.* It is not the task of biblical scholars to determine whether what religious persons said about God in the past is timelessly true. It *is* the job of biblical scholars to truthfully and accurately *interpret* what religious persons have said about God. In other words, when I am teaching a class, it is not my duty to prove that the Bible is the word of God. I may personally hold that belief, but it is not my task as a scholar to prove it. If students walk out of my classes without a definite conviction as to whether the Bible is the word of God, I do not count that as a failure. If, however, I have not helped my students understand what religious people in the past understood about God and the things of God, I count that as a failure.

Until approximately five hundred years ago, biblical interpretation was the sole territory of academics and ecclesiastics, who were always under the authority of the church. The only place people regularly heard the Bible was in church, largely because Bibles were not readily available to the average person. In the sixteenth century, however, two revolutions completely changed the landscape of biblical interpretation: the invention of the printing press and the Protestant Reformation. The printing press made it possible for more people than ever before to own Bibles and read them at home. The Protestant Reformation advanced that personal Bible study by advocating a doctrine known as the priesthood of all believers. The idea of the priesthood of all believers is that just as every Christian has an inner liberty of conscience that makes him or her a "lord over all," so, too, every Christian is a priest or "servant of all." By this, Martin Luther (1483–1546) meant not simply that every person has his or her own direct access to Christ, but that all Christians are "worthy to appear before God to pray for others and to teach one another the things of God." The practical application of this doctrine means that church authority does not bind or limit people when it comes to the interpretation of scripture.

The Reformation was responsible for the accessibility of the Bible in another way as well. During this time the translation of the biblical texts from the language of scholars (i.e., Latin and Greek) to the everyday language of the common person was begun. The widely used King James Version of the Bible was one of the fruits of these revolutions in biblical accessibility.

A Note on the History of Biblical Research

Biblical criticism is a very general term, and not an easy one to define because it covers a wide range of scholarly activities. Its roots are found in the linguistic and literary character of the Bible itself. Scripture was written in human languages (Hebrew, Aramaic, and Greek), and it uses the patterns of human expression, which can be interpreted only by means of human understanding. God may speak through scripture, but the meaning of the text occurs within the structures of ordinary human language. Biblical research takes the Bible very seriously and moves from the language of a particular text, such as a verse or selection of verses, to larger, overarching themes found, scholars believe, in the particular document itself. Approached in this way, the Bible is sometimes found to have meanings other than those that traditional or cursory (i.e., hasty) interpretations have suggested. In this way, biblical criticism is "critical," not in the sense that it "criticizes" the Bible, but in the sense that it *carefully* and *deliberately* engages the text and assumes the freedom to derive from the Bible meanings that may differ from those that traditional religion has seen in it. Biblical criticism may raise new questions about a text, even as it offers fresh answers in place of old solutions. (Note: In this discussion I shall use the terms "scholarship," "criticism," and "research" interchangeably.)

The purpose of biblical research is not to challenge traditional understandings of the Bible, but sometimes that is the result. Research may show a traditional interpretation to have been ill-grounded in scripture. For example, it may suggest a new interpretation based on the evidence discovered. Biblical research has at times upset proponents of existing religion; yet such disturbance is necessary to any viable belief in biblical authority. When reading the text, scholars momentarily suspend their acceptance of the existing interpretation to see whether it stands the test of interrogation against the biblical material itself.

Not surprisingly, religious conflict has been an important stimulus to critical questioning. Various groups may share the same sacred text but have widely differing interpretations of it. Each side appeals to the Bible and argues that it cannot mean what others have taken it to mean. Against, for example, the Christian understanding of Isaiah 7:14 as a prediction of Christ's virgin birth, the Jew Trypho, in the second century C.E., insisted that the Hebrew word "alma" means simply "young woman," that no virgin birth is involved, and that the reference is to the natural birth of King Hezekiah. The religious conflicts and disagreements that most stimulated the rise of modern biblical criticism were, initially, the Catholic-Protestant disagreements and, later, the disputes among the different groups within Protestantism. These debates emphasized the distinctive role of scripture and the implications of reading it for and *from* itself. From these debates, the discipline of biblical criticism was born, but not without challenge, and from its beginning the discipline has had to respond to six perennial issues:

1. *Theologically presupposed ideas* or *principles* about the Bible, such as the conviction that, as the word of God, the Bible must necessarily be perfect and thus inerrant in all its parts. Against these theoretical convictions, criticism works with the factual realities of the Bible (see Rule of Thumb 1).

2. *Interpretations that harmonize* and universalize ideas and meanings throughout the Bible, obscuring differences between one part and another. Criticism notices these differences, for example, the varying resurrection accounts in the Gospels (see Rule of Thumb 1).

3. *Allegorical interpretations.* This method of interpretation takes the words of one passage of scripture and ascribes to them meanings that may be found elsewhere in the Bible but do not necessarily fit the context of the passage being studied. Criticism takes the specific context to be decisive (see Rule of Thumb 11).

4. *Failure to perceive the literary forms* of the texts, and, particularly, the failure to give weight to the silences of scripture or to be silent where scripture is silent. The Hebrew Bible, for example, does not say that Adam's disobedience is an explanation for evil, nor is there an accounting for the absence of any birth narrative in Mark (see Rules of Thumb 7 and 11).

5. *Reading into the text* contemporary meanings, ideas, and situations. For example, it is an error to understand the term "bishop" in the New Testament as identical with medieval episcopacy, or to understand the term "scripture" in 2 Timothy 3:16 as if it meant exactly the same set of books that make up the modern Bible. Biblical research insists on starting with the definitions or meanings the words had when they were written (see Rule of Thumb 2).

6. *Justifying arguments* that are intended to overcome discrepancies between texts. Some argue, for example, that since Jesus' ejection of merchants from the temple is placed early in his ministry in John's Gospel, but late in the other Gospels, the event happened several times. Biblical research suggests that the different placings of the story were for reasons of theological meaning within the Gospels (see Rule of Thumb 11).

The rise of biblical scholarship paralleled the development of scientific knowledge and the resulting changing ideas about the world in which we live, which developed during the Enlightenment. Scientific knowledge made it seem impossible that the world originated as recently as the date implied by the Bible's own chronology, for example. Debates also arose as to the factual accuracy of biblical depictions of miracles. In the end, biblical miracles are essentially beyond proof. That is, they cannot conclusively be verified or discredited. Biblical scholarship is not in principle skeptical about miracles, but because they are difficult to prove, scholarship leaves the question of their truth aside. Instead, the scholar concentrates on the *meaning* or *function* of the miracle story within the work of the writer. For this purpose, it is unnecessary either to defend or deny the reality of a miracle, for the process of understanding the meaning works in the same way in either case.

The scholarly mind-set, which has been conditioned by historical studies, has given biblical scholarship a historical appearance. History often has been looked to as the essential component in biblical research, even though biblical study's foundations actually rest in language and literary form. This emphasis on history occurred because the literature of the Bible stimulated discussions of issues that often could not be resolved without a historical account of what had taken place. Take, for example, the work of the German scholar Julius Wellhausen (1844–1918). Wellhausen paired Hebrew Bible sources, identified through linguistic and literary criteria, with the evidence of historical stages in the development of religious institutions in Israel. From this he produced a likely sequence and dating of the biblical books. Dating sources and setting them within the framework of accepted world history provides both a strong frame of reference for academic biblical study and a way in which evidence can be marshaled and ordered for discussion and evaluation.

Wellhausen demonstrated that the books we currently know as the Hebrew Bible were formed by the combination of four earlier sources. He labeled these sources the Yahwist, the Elohist, the Deuteronomist, and Q, which we now call the Priestly source. This insight provided a new framework for the history of Israel's religion, and it strongly suggested that the religion of the "Jews" after the Babylonian exile was different from the religion of the Israelites before the exile. For example, the author(s) of Chronicles used Samuel-Kings, revising its sources sometimes slightly, sometimes drastically, and adding new material. In New Testament study, Mark is most commonly believed to have been used and rewritten by Matthew and Luke. In some cases the sources used have long since disappeared. For instance, the writer(s) of Kings mention historical sources known to them but not included in the Bible. Material common to Matthew and Luke, but absent from Mark, *could* go back to a source now lost (called Q or *Quelle* [German for "source"] by scholars). In the Pentateuch, the first five books of the Bible, what some scholars see as different literary perspectives, each marked by very different language, style, and ideas, could be explained if a variety of sources from different times had been gradually combined and edited. The fact that different sources were used within the same book may help explain the discrepancies and divergent theological viewpoints found in it. This type of approach to the biblical texts, called *source criticism,* is characteristic of biblical research. It, along with studying questions of authorship and date, is sometimes called "higher criticism." In contrast, "lower criticism" means the study of texts and textual variations. In some circles today these terms are considered old-fashioned. Certain scholars argue that questions of authorship, date, and sources have been settled, and that biblical scholarship needs to move on to other areas of research, such as the overall effect of a biblical passage on the reader. Nevertheless, the great majority of scholars continue use source-critical questions and results as the basic framework for discussion, and the broad outlines of source identification in the key areas of biblical scholarship are widely accepted.

The centrality of the historical enterprise, with the importance of the perspective it affords scholars, has often mistakenly caused all biblical research to be understood as "historical criticism." This viewpoint, unfortunately, exaggerates the degree to which the ideals of historical research dominate biblical study. *Historical investigation is only one of the methods of biblical interpretation.* Much critical work is basically the interpretation of biblical books; for this, complete historical precision is often impossible. Determining the general historical context is more important than complete historical accuracy. To avoid the distortion of anachronism, the biblical scholar must understand words to mean what they meant in the language of the texts, in the time of the texts. Texts must be seen against the situation in life for which they were written.

In reality, however, biblical scholars, even when they insist on a historical approach, are not necessarily very historical. That is, they do not always adhere to the principles of research laid down in the general study of history. They too often let theology eclipse history in their study of the Bible, and they are often moved by devotion to texts more than by pure historical rigor. Initially, traditional theology advocated an emphasis on what "really happened" in biblical times, on the persons behind the writings, and on history as the context of God's activity (see Rule of Thumb 19). So the historical perspective on the Bible that biblical research has brought about is important primarily as a major fact within theology itself, rather than as a purely historical achievement.

One important aspect of this historical investigation is the scholarly perception of the canon of scripture: *the canon came about historically and can be understood historically.* In biblical studies, the canon is that group of texts, commonly called scripture, that is deemed authoritative by a faith community. For Protestants, the twenty-seven books that constitute the New Testament and the thirty-nine books that constitute the Hebrew Bible or Old Testament are called the canon. As you might guess, the canon is important because it is deemed the authoritative source for theology and ethics (see the discussion on "The Creation of the Bible Itself," below). The early studies of Johann Semler (1725–91) in this area were a vital step in the development of modern biblical scholarship. The boundaries of scripture are not something eternally and unchangeably established by God; what constituted scripture at one given time was not identical with its definition at another time. This means that if one is to understand the Bible properly, the study of scripture and the study of the history of the religious institution that created the canon, such as the church, are inseparable. The formation of the canon can be understood as inspired, just as the contents of scripture are inspired, but not purely and supernaturally so. The inspiration of the Bible, that is, the movement of God that caused certain people to accept some writings as sacred and to reject others, occurs only indirectly, through the mediation of human arrangements and meanings. Biblical scholars do not reject the canon. Rather they uphold it, maintaining that the religious content of the Bible has, through the process of canonization, proven to have greater meaning to the life of a faith community than other contenders to religious authority.

Central to biblical scholarship is its acknowledgment that biblical books do not share one consistent theological view and emphasis. The Bible is not a monochromatic and unvarying account of the being and will of God. In spite of much common subject matter, Matthew, for example, presents a picture of Jesus quite different from Luke's. While this in itself is no revolutionary insight, it is a valuable tool to identify sources and their relative dating, situations, and problems. Similarly, biblical scholarship strives to distinguish, understand, and evaluate these different theological views as crucial stages in the understanding of scripture as a whole.

Biblical scholarship may appear to be something new, but, in reality, it has ancient theological roots. Interest in authorship goes back to second-century biblical research and was part of the argument in the church about canonicity. From early times, an author's writing style was used as a criterion for canonicity. On the basis of style, John

Calvin doubted that the apostle Peter had written 2 Peter. Likewise, the emphasis on history was also part of general Christian tradition: Christians have thought of Christianity as a peculiarly historical religion and have always stressed the importance of determining the actual words and deeds of Jesus. If biblical scholarship noted and explained the theological differences within the Bible, this was only an extension of the practice of theology. Theologians have always, even when accepting the total canon of scripture, identified various portions as more essential and dominant than others. For example Martin Luther, driven by his theological position, effectively demoted from the New Testament the books of James, Hebrews (which he believed was not written by Paul), and Revelation, because of their inadequate understanding of justification by faith through grace.

As I noted earlier, the Reformation fueled the rise of biblical scholarship. By stressing scripture alone (called the principle of *sola scriptura*), all theology and doctrine appeared dependent on scripture. The Reformers' focus on the grammar and wording of the "original text" required a learned ministry capable of handling these words. The Reformers rejected what they considered nonliteral methods of interpretation (e.g., allegorical interpretation) that covered over cracks in the surface of scripture in order to make scripture conform to church teaching. The Reformers asserted the freedom of the interpreter to take a stand on the biblical words and against traditional interpretations. Yet, despite the Reformers' insistence on biblical authority, they failed to resolve doctrinal disagreement. On the contrary, they created a wide variety of conflicting doctrinal positions, all claiming a basis in scripture. The wide variation of ideas and hypotheses within later biblical criticism reflects the same situation.

Yes, there were ancient and early modern anticipations of modern biblical research, but they are not in themselves important for us, because our focus here is on modern biblical interpretation. More important than the precursors was the growth of an environment in which a scholar was free to argue about the basis of the language and literary form of scripture and to offer novel interpretations that emerged from this discussion. This tradition of questioning more than likely goes back to the Renaissance thinker Erasmus (1466–1536), and was continued by others, such as the Dutchman Hugo Grotius (1583–1645). Still others, like Richard Simon (1638–1712) in France, argued that uncertainties about scripture undermined the Protestant reliance upon it, while freedom in biblical study produced no clash with Catholic teaching. Jean Astruc (1684–1766), also a Frenchman, pioneered the systematic source analysis of the Pentateuch and viewed the different documents as initially isolated but combined by Moses himself—a position that was later undermined by Wellhausen.

Seventeenth- and eighteenth-century England was fertile ground for new ideas about scripture. Diverse viewpoints about church polity, civil government, and religious freedom all sought legitimation from scripture. The resulting controversies were catalysts for even newer ideas and arguments. Important insights came from philosophers like John Locke (1632–1704), who noted, among other things, how Jesus kept secret his messianic status until late in his career. Even Sir Isaac Newton (1642–1727), better known for his scientific research, worked on biblical chronology and believed that a close reading of the New Testament could disprove the idea of the Trinity.

In the later eighteenth century, German university professors applied these close readings of the text in a more systematic way. Their scholarship typically took the form of a written "introduction," which covered in turn each book of the Hebrew Bible or New Testament and discussed methodically, on the basis of language and content, all matters of authorship, source analysis, and dates. A pioneer in such work was Johann Eichhorn, whose five-volume *Introduction to the New Testament* was published between 1804 and 1827. Other names bear mention. In Hebrew Bible scholarship Wilhelm Martin Leberecht de Wette (1780–1849) is noted for his work on the book of Deuteronomy, and Julius Wellhausen, mentioned above, whose solution (the "P" document is the latest of the Pentateuchal sources) remains the point of reference for all discussion of the subject. In New Testament studies, Ferdinand Christian Baur (1792–1860) determined that a conflict between Pauline and Petrine traditions was decisive for early Christianity. And the claim of Johannes Weiss (1863–1914) that Jesus' mission was dominated by the expectation of the impending end of the world is crucial to any discussion of the topic today.

As you can imagine, the development of modern biblical scholarship was not without conflict among both academics and churchgoers. For example, W. Robertson Smith was removed from his professorship in Scotland in 1881, and Charles A. Briggs from his ministerial functions in the United States in 1893, because of the controversy surrounding critical biblical scholarship. Nonetheless, modern biblical scholarship secured its place as a respectable academic enterprise. By the early twentieth century, critical interpretations were accepted, though not always easily, in both academic study and serious publishing throughout the Western non–Roman Catholic world.

Among Roman Catholics, Richard Simon argued that critical freedom favored the Catholic position, but this was rarely if ever accepted, and critical Roman Catholic biblical scholarship was muted until the rise of Catholic modernism in the late nineteenth and early twentieth centuries. The so-called modernist movement was formally condemned by Pius X in 1907, but since the 1943 papal encyclical (i.e., a papal letter) *Divino afflante spiritu,* and especially since the Second Vatican

Council, the critical freedom of the Catholic biblical scholar has been acknowledged, and today Catholic and Protestant biblical scholarship generally form one total constituency.

Although biblical scholarship clearly led many academics, ministers, and even laypersons to read the Bible differently, it did not have the destructive effects on doctrine that some feared. This was primarily because many traditional doctrines were not as dependent on the Bible as had been supposed. Changes in the understanding of the Bible actually made it possible for these doctrines to be maintained. For example, modern biblical study did not undermine the Protestant understanding of the necessity of the scriptures for salvation, that is, the understanding that the Bible contains all the information necessary for salvation. Some Christians believed that there was only one proper way to be a disciple of Jesus Christ. Biblical scholarship pointed out that even in the New Testament itself one can find different understandings of what it means to follow Jesus. Indeed, biblical scholarship fit well with certain important doctrinal emphases: justification by faith in Lutheranism, the centrality of incarnation in Anglicanism, the appreciation of Israel and the Hebrew Bible in Calvinism.

Jewish academic scholarship has often disagreed with the solutions of Christian scholarship; examples include opposition to Wellhausen's source criticism regarding the Pentateuch. Jewish scholars have felt that non-Jewish scholarship has been overly influenced by Christian theological traditions and, as a result, have viewed with suspicion Christian scholarship on the Hebrew Bible. The positions advanced by Jewish scholars for understanding the Hebrew Bible are in their own way just as critical. Jewish scholarship takes the Hebrew Bible seriously, and it promotes a very close reading of the text based on its own distinctive method of interpretation.

The emphasis on scholarly evaluation has created a situation in which biblical scholarship has often been understood primarily as a nontheological discipline. This is not totally accurate, for biblical scholarship is inextricably linked with the discipline of biblical theology. Biblical theology seeks the common elements that run through the texts, whether through a historical or developmental scheme or through the perception of an inner structure. Biblical theology, like criticism, is an exploratory approach: the theology of the Bible is not self-evident, but must be discovered. For the opponents of modern biblical scholarship, the theology of scripture is already known, fixed in often ancient creeds and traditions. Though twentieth-century biblical theology sometimes feels itself to be in conflict with biblical criticism, theology and criticism are in fact two sides of the same coin. Both are in search of the truth of the text, although that search takes different directions when carried out in an academic environment. The goal of biblical theology is to make general statements regarding the Bible, or parts of it, while biblical criticism tries to avoid making general statements in favor of concentrating on the distinctiveness of biblical texts.

Returning to the Aims of Biblical Study

Biblical studies—one of the oldest disciplines in the academic community—uses the same methods to ascertain the truth as any other discipline. Being part of an academic community means acknowledging that there are accepted methods of research in the academy and that the study of religion must abide by those methods. This idea of accepted methods of research is not without its detractors, and controversies abound as to what acceptable research methods should be.

However, this is not the problem that confronts the student. The problem for many students is that they see religion, particularly biblical studies, as embodying eternally self-evident truths, while the academics with whom they are studying do not always share this belief. Academics see it as their job to search and re-search for the truth. This means using certain methods or tools for distinguishing between truth and falsehood. There are degrees and means by which one can discern the truthfulness of a proposition, and being part of an academic community means that scholars to varying degrees have accepted these methods by which we distinguish between truth and error.

To summarize, the aims of Bible study and the aims of biblical scholarship are different, although not mutually exclusive. Academic biblical scholarship is more interested in determining what a particular text *meant* to its first readers and how that meaning has been maintained or modified through successive generations. This does not mean that biblical scholars do not care about the meaning of the scriptures in our day, but that it is not their *primary* concern. Bible study—the kind that goes on in churches, clubs, and dorm rooms—is more interested in determining what a particular text *means* for "me" and "my" present faith journey. Many people who participate in Bible studies are concerned with understanding all they can about the history and probable original meaning of a text, but this also is not their *primary* concern.

Methods of Biblical Interpretation

Up to this point in our discussion of biblical scholarship, we have focused on the method of interpretation known as the historical-critical method. This is the foundational method of modern biblical scholarship, but by no means the only method. There are almost as many ways of understanding and interpreting the Bible as there are biblical scholars. Yet, in spite of the diversity in the field of interpretation, certain methods have been dominant. I will outline a few of these.

Form Criticism

Form criticism began in the 1920s. This method looks at smaller literary units and attempts (1) to determine their "setting in life," in order, (2) based on that setting, to determine the underlying purpose for the creation of the unit. Let's use Mark 2:15–17, as an example:

> And as he sat at dinner in Levi's house, many tax collectors and sinners were also sitting with Jesus and his disciples—for there were many who followed him. When the scribes of the Pharisees saw that he was eating with sinners and tax collectors, they said to his disciples, "Why does he eat with tax collectors and sinners?" When Jesus heard this, he said to them, "Those who are well have no need of a physician, but those who are sick; I have come to call not the righteous but sinners."

Form criticism classifies this incident as some sort of "controversy dialogue," which means that the scene itself is not as important as the controversy that underlies it. The form critic is not interested in whether or not this scene actually occurred. In fact, a number of questions arise when one tries to argue for the historicity of the scene. How did the scribes of the Pharisees "see" that Jesus was eating at Levi's house when, presumably, the group would have been eating inside? Who was Jesus talking to in his response, the disciples or the scribes? And, if it was the scribes, how did he hear what they were saying when he was inside?

Instead, what concerns the form critic is what this controversy between Jews and "Christians" means. The scene demonstrates the early Christian conviction that Jews (in this case the Pharisees) are not really concerned with helping those who really need to be helped, namely, sinners. It also demonstrates that Christians are drawing their members from groups of people with questionable moral character—prostitutes and sinners—and are being criticized for this practice. Thus, this scene provides a Christian argument for including undesirable persons in their religious community, even while those same persons would have been rejected by the Jewish religious community.

Form criticism enables us, among other things, to distinguish in the Hebrew Bible between different types of psalms and to assign them to what we believe to be appropriate occasions in the worship life of Israel. Psalm 24, for example, is believed to have been a hymn used in a liturgical procession entering the Jerusalem temple:

> The earth is Yahweh's and all that is in it,
>> the world, and those who live in it;
> for he has founded it on the seas,
>> and established it on the rivers.
> Who shall ascend the hill of Yahweh?
>> And who shall stand in his holy place?
> Those who have clean hands and pure hearts,
>> who do not lift up their souls to what is false,
>> and do not swear deceitfully.
> They will receive blessing from Yahweh,
>> and vindication from the God of their salvation.
> Such is the company of those who seek him,
>> who seek the face of the God of Jacob.
> Lift up your heads, O gates!
>> and be lifted up, O ancient doors!
>> that the King of glory may come in.
> Who is the King of glory?
>> Yahweh, strong and mighty,
>> Yahweh, mighty in battle.
> Lift up your heads, O gates!
>> and be lifted up, O ancient doors!
>> that the King of glory may come in.
> Who is this King of glory?
>> Yahweh of hosts,
>> he is the King of glory!

(NSRV, replacing "the LORD" with "Yahweh")

The form critic attempts to identify the "setting in life" of the psalm in order to help us understand how the psalm was used and, therefore, what it means. Imagine priests carrying the ark of the covenant—the symbol of the presence of God—into the Temple welcomed by this psalm extolling God's glory!

Important practitioners of form criticism were Hermann Gunkel in Hebrew Bible and Rudolf Bultmann in New Testament. Many believe that New Testament form criticism has always had a cynical edge to it—as in the example above of Mark 2:15–17, where the issue was not whether Jesus actually spoke these words, but what the purpose for generating this kind of story would be. As noted, the purpose of this story may have been to justify the Christian church's practice of including undesirables in its religious community. In contrast, in the study of the Hebrew Bible, form criticism has tended to be rather conservative, suggesting ways in which poems and stories may have functioned in the life of ancient Israel.

Tradition Criticism

Tradition criticism seeks to illuminate the underlying forces that have molded the Bible into its present form. It concentrates on the way in which theological traditions in the Bible, such as the Yahwistic tradition, developed and matured, the places to which these traditions are attached, and the social and worship relations within which they have been meaningful. These traditions have been passed down in the form of stories, sayings, songs, poems, confessions, creeds, and the like. In many ways, tradition criticism is related to form criticism. But while form criticism seeks to identify small literary units like the psalm quoted above, tradition criticism seeks to chart the development of traditions behind these units.

In the Hebrew Bible, for example, one of the most widespread traditions concerns Israelite redemption from

Egypt. The exodus theme and the tradition of being led out of Egypt occur in narratives, psalms, and prophetic books. The theme of exile and return was a tradition that could be used in various contexts. Hosea depicts the ruin of the nation as a return to Egypt, while Isaiah 40–55 presents the return from exile as a new exodus. One of the earliest traces of the tradition involving the exodus can be found in Deuteronomy 26:5–9:

> A wandering Aramean was my ancestor; he went down into Egypt and lived there as an alien, few in number, and there he became a great nation, mighty and populous. When the Egyptians treated us harshly and afflicted us, by imposing hard labor on us, we cried to Yahweh, the God of our ancestors; Yahweh heard our voice and saw our affliction, our toil, and our oppression. Yahweh brought us out of Egypt with a mighty hand and an outstretched arm, with a terrifying display of power, and with signs and wonders; and he brought us into this land, a land flowing with milk and honey.
>
> (NRSV, replacing "the LORD" with "Yahweh")

These and other traditions found in the Hebrew Bible, like the traditions about wandering in the wilderness and the conquest of Canaan, demonstrate the continuation and expansion of Israelite ideas about significant events in their history.

In the New Testament, numerous examples can be taken from the Gospels to illustrate the importance of understanding the history of traditions, for example, the traditions about Jesus' birth, his baptism, and his triumphal entry into Jerusalem. Among the Pauline writings 1 Corinthians 15:1–11 demonstrates the point about the development of tradition. It is now widely agreed among scholars that verses 3–5 consist of a pre-Pauline summary of Christian preaching, or at least one version of it: "For I *handed on to you* as of first importance what I in turn *had received:* that Christ died for our sins in accordance with the scriptures, and that he was buried, and that he was raised on the third day in accordance with the scriptures, and that he appeared to the twelve" (1 Cor. 15:3–5, emphasis mine). Scholars have reached this conclusion by noting that Paul refers to handing on to the Corinthians what he himself received (i.e., a tradition) and that Paul uses terms in this discussion that are either unusual for him or, at least, not used by him elsewhere in his writings. Thus, scholars have concluded that here Paul is transmitting a tradition that belonged to the early church.

Redaction Criticism

Redaction criticism, also known as editorial criticism, is concerned with the work of the final editor(s), who worked or reworked the earlier sources into the text that we now possess. Redaction criticism presupposes and relies on the insights of form criticism and tradition criticism. The redaction critical method depends on these previously determined views of the sources used by the final editor(s), but the interest is less on the sources themselves than on the way the sources have been adapted into the final version of the text. For example, instead of trying to harmonize the differences between the Gospels of Matthew, Mark, and Luke, redaction criticism seeks to let each account—which means each editor—speak for itself, because its thesis is that the differences that arise in the final versions of the account are significant. Thus, the goal of redaction criticism is to understand the shape and structure of the book as we now have it.

A good example of how redaction criticism looks at the Hebrew Bible is in 1 and 2 Kings. The Deuteronomic editor makes references to his sources in his version of the text: "the book of the acts of Solomon" (1 Kings 11:41), "the Book of the Annals of the Kings of Israel" (1 Kings 14:19), and "the Book of the Annals of the Kings of Judah" (1 Kings 14:29). Drawing from these sources—and possibly others—the editor developed a new work that contained his own theological evaluation of the monarchs that reigned in the land of Canaan. Redaction criticism sees the editor as a creative theologian who used his sources and edited them in order to suit his own purposes. The job of the practitioner of this method is to understand how the biblical editor(s) combined sources and to emphasize the importance of the entirety of the work; to understand not just the individual parts, as in form and tradition criticisms, but what the editor is trying to say by arranging the traditions as a single whole.

When it comes to the New Testament, the concerns of various redactors (or editors) can be seen by looking at the first three Gospels: Matthew, Mark, and Luke. These Gospels are called the Synoptic Gospels. (The term "synopsis" means "seeing together.") The Synoptic Gospels often report the same event, episode, or saying but in different versions. Academic study of the Gospels has enabled us to place the Synoptics on a rough historical continuum, and this continuum allows us to determine how Mark, Matthew, and Luke used their sources and adapted them in order to make their particular theological points. For example, the scene describing Jesus' death on the cross (Matt. 27:45–56; Mark 15:33–41; Luke 2:44–49) highlights the differences in the editors' understandings of the event. When you look at the accounts carefully, you see that each editor gives a distinctive spin or profile to the scene. In fact, no two are identical. Matthew's account is longer than Mark's, while Luke's is conspicuously shorter. Scholars believe that Matthew redacted (that is, edited) Mark by expanding on it, and Luke redacted by abbreviating. Redaction can be seen in specific points, as well. For example, according to Matthew, after Jesus' death, besides the tearing of the veil of the temple, there is an earthquake that results in saints being resurrected. This incident does not appear either in Mark or Luke.

Literary Critical Methods of Interpretation

As redaction criticism indicates (and as noted earlier in our discussion on the history of biblical interpretation), the literary character of the Bible is very important to biblical scholarship. However, since the 1960s there has been a growing feeling among biblical scholars that methods of biblical interpretation are out of step with modern trends in the study of literature. Literary critics, such as Frank Kermode, Robert Alter, and Northrop Frye, who work outside of formal biblical scholarship, have made meaningful contributions to biblical interpretation, and recent biblical scholars have been following their lead. Most of this movement in biblical interpretation—like redaction criticism—is concerned with the final form of the text and not its historical reconstruction. Literary criticism is concerned with the styles, the patterns, and the narrative techniques that go into the creation of a text. This mode of interpretation has been less concerned with the theological issues than have other forms of biblical interpretation, like redaction criticism, which focuses on the theological viewpoint of the text's author. Some literary critics think that the text does not "refer" to anything outside itself at all (i.e., to some actual historical circumstance), but operates within a certain world of its own—usually called "the world of the text."

Literary criticism overlaps in some ways with *structuralism,* another method used by some scholars to read the biblical text. Structuralism, which began in France, is interested in the linguistic codes, the set of structures, that are used in all communicative processes and that serve to give the text a "foundation of meaning." (That is, the linguistic structures give the biblical text a way to be interpreted, but that way of interpreting the text is not understood to be the only way to interpret it.) In structuralism, the emphasis is on the synchronic (i.e., the structures visible within one text at one given time) rather than on the diachronic (i.e., the development of structures over a span of time), although some structuralist interpretations do attempt to deal with historical change. Structuralism brackets out the author, the original audience, and the historical setting—all of which form the basis of historical criticism. It makes no attempt to answer, or be concerned with, the traditional questions: Who wrote it? To whom was it written? When? Where? How? Why? Under what circumstances? Rather, structuralists argue that whatever meaning is being conveyed is not conveyed from an author through the text, but from the text itself.

In general, such literary reading of the Bible differs greatly from traditional biblical scholarship, which has been more concerned with historical reconstruction. Literary criticism offers us a keen insight into the "world of the text," while it leaves the "world outside the text" to other methods of interpretation.

Canonical Criticism

Scholars such as Brevard S. Childs have advanced the form of criticism known as canonical criticism, an even more recent method of interpretation. This method insists that the canon of scripture is the essential key to interpretation. Canonical criticism is interested in the final text, not in the earlier stages that have led up to it. The canon of books, which has been brought together as the holy scriptures, is the foundational document that regulates the faith and life of the community. Viewed as "the canon," the biblical books provide an explanation of all of their contents. Canonical critics use traditional biblical scholarship as the point of departure for reasoning toward the Bible's canonical sense. Although canonical criticism appears to draw from other methods of biblical interpretation, such as redaction criticism, Childs is anxious to disclaim that connection, arguing that canonical criticism is not literary in character but theological, because it starts from the theological determination of the Bible as scripture.

Postmodern Biblical Criticism

Postmodern biblical interpretation is based on a method of reading literature known as *deconstruction,* which derives its insights from structuralism, discussed above. The central problem in understanding postmodern interpretation and deconstruction lies in the inability of even its practitioners to define it. In fact, the first thing one can say about deconstruction is that it sees the word "is" as problematic. Deconstruction challenges our most basic assumptions about the world and how we understand it. It identifies this as the problem of "presence" or "identity," or as Jacques Derrida, a deconstructionist, refers to it, "logocentrism." The problem of "presence" is the presumption that our words refer to something out there (a thing, idea, or concept) that has a reality. Deconstruction questions whether we really know what is out there at all. Deconstruction, in its own words, *decenters* the word from its central place in human conversation and thought. It does not deny that words have meanings, but it recognizes that those meanings are always determined in relationship to other words and their meanings. Identity, the philosophical concept upon which we base our idea that words have meaning, is a human creation that decides that one can determine a difference between "this" and "that." Identity occurs when one decides that certain distinctions make a difference and others do not.

Building upon the deconstructive insight regarding identity, postmodern critics challenge three assumptions that underlie modern thinking.

1. Postmodern critics challenge the modern assumptions that reason is king and that human history is a constant march toward progress. The central characteristic of

modern thinking is that rationalism and scientific inquiry are the proper and most desirable ways to think. In fact, the idea of the modern university is based precisely upon this scientific characteristic. The result of this mind-set is that modern thinking privileges people with credentials over those without them. Credentialed people, called professionals, have advanced and specialized knowledge in certain areas of investigation, such as history, biology, and religion. Specialized knowledge gives professionals a certain authority over nonprofessionals. In the field of religion, professionals, such as biblical scholars and ministers, are given greater authority to interpret the Bible than are laypersons. Postmodern criticism calls such authority into question and declares that the interpretations of professionals are not better (or worse) than those of nonprofessionals. They are just different.

2. Postmodern critics challenge the assumption that there is at least one indubitable truth. The modern idea that there is such a truth comes from, among other things, a famous statement made by the French philosopher René Descartes: "I think, therefore I am." The one thing Descartes could be absolutely sure existed was himself. Philosophically, this means that there is such a thing as "reality" (that is, an incontestable foundation upon which all other forms of knowledge can build). Whether one accepts Descartes's idea, or one believes the foundation of reality to be the existence of God or the innate equality of human beings, postmodern critics point out that it is a characteristic of modern thinking to *assume* that such a foundation exists. Postmodern critics shun ideas that aspire to be universal truths (that is, reality), in fact, they deny the existence of universals, whether theories or rules, and argue rather for particular "local" truths derived from specific cases of investigation. Along with this postmodern understanding that there are only "local" truths, postmodern critics do not claim any privileged access to

the truth. What they offer instead is a provocative under-standing of the topics they engage.

3. Postmodern critics challenge the assumption that one can determine an author's intention. Determining what an author intended is the single most important measure modern scholars use in deciding the legitimacy of a textual interpretation. In contrast, postmodern critics argue that the identity of the author, or the author's inten-tion, is as unstable as any other foundation upon which to build an argument. Authorial intention, like identity, involves making distinctions about what is important and what is not, and those distinctions are made by later inter-preters. In short, postmodern critics point out that we do not have access to the author's intention in writing a text, but only to the interpreter's idea of what the author intended, an idea that may or may not be correct.

We can identify at least four ways in which postmodern thought has changed the discipline of biblical studies.

1. For postmodern critics, there is no absolute reference point upon which we can orient our interpretations. One cannot locate the world *behind* the text (as in historical criti-cism), or the world *of* the text (as in certain forms of literary criticism), or the world *in front of* the text (as in a method of interpretation known as reader-response criticism). They also discourage any talk of extracting meaning *from* the text. To the contrary, they hold that meaning is what we make of texts, not an ingredient in texts. This means that all interpre-tations of a biblical passage are potentially legitimate read-ings of the text. No special privilege or authority can be given to the interpretations of scholars and educated minis-ters as they meet interpretations of laypeople in a Wednes-day evening Bible study class.

2. Postmodern critics caution that to try to overcome the relational limits of language is to fail. As I noted

before, language is constructed on the basis of identity, and this involves distinctions and exclusions. Exclusions rest on the pairing of two terms/concepts, of which one is normative ("this"), and the other derivative, or less-than-the-first ("that"). For instance, when Genesis 2:23b says, "This one shall be called Woman [*ishshah*], for out of Man [*ish*] this one was taken," the message is clear: man is primary, woman secondary. A value judgment has been made regarding the relative importance of the female human being. At the same time, critics point out that the term "man" is meaningless unless it is paired with the excluded second term, "woman." All language is caught up in such relationships, and human beings privilege one term over the other by determining that certain distinctions do make a difference.

Postmodern critics insist that there will always be traces of exclusions and the distinctions that do not make a difference in the use of language, which a careful reader can locate and use to undermine the concept of identity. By way of illustration, take the term "Christian" as an expression of identity. Although no one in the New Testament calls himself or herself a Christian, later interpreters, such as ourselves, have drawn a distinction between certain people who claimed that "Jesus is Lord" and those who did not, namely, Jews and pagans. Postmodern critics point out that the term "Christian" is meaningless unless it is related to the excluded terms Jew and pagan, and that any attempt to define Christian without reference to Jew and pagan is doomed to failure. Furthermore, critics maintain that the privileged status accorded the term "Christian" results from the (Christian) decision that this is a distinction that makes a difference.

3. Postmodern critics shatter universals by deconstructing identity. A case in point is the academic debate surrounding the authenticity of Paul's letters—did Paul actually write this or that letter? A debate has raged since

certain scholars (e.g., J. E. C. Schmidt in 1798 regarding 2 Thessalonians) claimed that some letters attributed to Paul are authentic (that is, written by Paul during the course of his ministry) and others are inauthentic (that is, written by someone imitating Paul's style of writing, usually assumed to have been done after Paul's death). The key issue revolves around successfully determining the identity of the author of the letters. In the argument about 2 Thessalonians, those who advocate Pauline authorship point out that this letter uses much of the same vocabulary as 1 Thessalonians, while those who deny Pauline authorship suspect that such similarities mean that the author of 2 Thessalonians was consciously imitating the style of 1 Thessalonians.

Postmodern critics question the use of the terms "authentic/inauthentic," with the privileged status going to the letter deemed to be authentic. They point out that the same evidence can be used by both sides of the argument, and that the issue of authorship is ultimately undecidable. In addition, they question the validity of authenticity as a foundation for research on Paul. When authenticity is displaced as the foundation for an interpretation of the Pauline letters, the issue of the author's identity loses its importance.

4. Postmodern criticism allows interpreters to interact with texts in novel ways. Deconstruction suggests that there are no unnatural ways to interpret texts. Therefore, deconstruction has played an important role in persuading some interpreters that all interpretation is political. This political criticism, usually called *ideological criticism,* begins with the Marxist insight that societies operate under certain ideologies that allow people to make sense of a (sometimes) chaotic world. Biblical ideological critics aim at stripping the Bible of its "religious" aura by pointing out how the Bible participates in, and has been used as a tool for, ideological conflict.

Ideology can mean different things to different interpreters, but there are at least three prominent understandings of ideology at work in biblical criticism. (a) Some interpreters define ideology as a misleading justification of social practices that are inherently oppressive. It is found first and foremost in the assertion that "that's just how things are." These interpreters believe that such ideologies privilege some individuals above others: men over women, whites over blacks, rich over poor, and Christian over Jew. When these interpreters look at the Bible, they look for ways in which the Bible justifies (or argues against) the subjugation of some for the benefit of others. The ideological critic Norman Gottwald, in his 1979 book *The Tribes of Yahweh*, for instance, claims that a group of people, who came to be called Israel, began a haphazard revolution against Canaanite feudal authority, which is documented in the books of Joshua and Judges, and that the religious justification for this revolution was added later. (b) Other interpreters define ideology as any set of political goals and assumptions, similar to the idea of a "political agenda." Critics of ideological criticism most often use this understanding of ideology, which ignores some of the real social conditions that are at the heart of such criticism. (c) Still other interpreters define ideology as a description of *all* the social interactions that ascribe "significance" to human behavior. They point out that ideology is not just a tool for privileging some over others, but that all human consciousness is rooted in an ideology (for instance, the conviction that all human beings are innately equal and that this equality confers on humans certain inalienable "rights"). In this case, ideology is a component of all interpretation, and ideological critics in this vein often point out that "academic objectivity" is a charade. They may note that the scholar's ability to think about such grand abstractions as "history" or "religion," and to insist on his or her own "objectivity," is rooted in the scholar's privileged social status. Scholars, unlike many others in society, do not have to concern themselves with the day-to-day problem of "making ends meet," and so they have the necessary free time to reflect on such things. Scholarly authority is undergirded by the ideological justification that one needs academic credentials in order to speak intelligently on such matters, which itself requires that one have the free time necessary to pursue such an education.

As this brief overview indicates, biblical scholarship is a dynamic field of study. New methods and perspectives continue to arise, and old areas of study continue to be looked at anew. Scholars are, for example, reexaming such topics as the character of Judaism at the time Christianity began and the character of scripture as story rather than as history. Scholars now understand that first-century Judaism was more diverse than formerly was thought, that Judaism in Palestine, during and after the time of Jesus, was not the coherent, rabbi-led religion that it is today. These methods offer new insights into the biblical document, yet, for the most part, they function well within the continuity of traditional forms of biblical interpretation.

A Primer on Biblical Basics

The Creation of the Bible Itself

The Bible is a collection of books deemed important for a faith community that developed over time and from two main linguistic traditions. The books that eventually became the Bible were not initially books at all. Most were originally written on scrolls made of leather or papyrus, a kind of "paper" made from a fibrous Egyptian plant. The codex, which had pages and was similar to modern books, first appeared in the first century C.E. It was superior to the scroll because it could be enlarged simply by adding pages, and it was easier to use, to work on, and to transport. The codex was popular among Christians and Jews, although Jews continue to use the scroll in official worship ceremonies.

Both the scroll and the codex were manually reproduced by one of two methods. (Remember, the printing press did not come into use until the sixteenth century.) In one method, a single scribe copied a manuscript by hand. In the other, a single scribe read a manuscript to a number of other scribes who recorded what they heard. The second method produced more copies in a shorter time, but the first was usually more accurate. Both methods, however, were prone to error. Scribes would get tired or bored with the tedious work of copying, and would misread, misunderstand, or omit words or entire lines. Thus, in spite of scribes' dedication to their work and efforts to eliminate mistakes, errors crept into the text (see Rule of Thumb 17). Beyond the problems of copying, the issue of the boundaries of scripture confronted the scribes: What should I copy as scripture?

Protestants are quick to say that there are only sixty-six books in the Bible, but that is not an objectively true statement. While the New Testament contains twenty-seven books, the number of books in the Hebrew Bible varies with one's vantage point. According to Jews, there are twenty-four books in the Hebrew Bible (the twelve "minor" prophets comprising one book). Roman Catholics hold that there are forty-six, the Orthodox that there are forty-four, and Protestants that there are thirty-nine. In short, the number of books in the Bible is a lot more complicated than the number of languages used in creating the scriptures.

The Languages of the Bible

Most of the Hebrew Bible was originally written in Hebrew. For a small part of it, Aramaic was used. Both languages are Semitic, which means they are written from right to left. The New Testament was written in Greek. The Hebrew Bible was translated into a Greek version known as the Septuagint, which was the primary version used by the early church. The biblical texts were translated into other languages as well, but they are not necessary topics for our purposes here.

Chapter and Verse Divisions

Although the ancients divided the Bible into literary units, we will concentrate on the system used today. Our modern chapter and verse divisions have sometimes been attributed to Cardinal Hugo of St. Cher (d. 1263), who developed a system for use in his concordance to the Vulgate, the Latin version of the Bible. Cardinal Hugo, however, had himself adopted, with small modifications, a system that had been introduced by Stephen Langton, a lecturer at the University of Paris who later became archbishop of Canterbury. The system consisted of subdividing the text into seven portions marked in the margin by the letters A through G.

The idea of numbering verses came from Rabbi Isaac Nathan about 1440 while he was working on a concordance to the Hebrew Bible. Rabbi Nathan used Hebrew numerals for the verses. Arabic numerals were first added to the text by Joseph Athias at Amsterdam in 1661. Robert Stephanus (Estienne) introduced the current verse division in the New Testament in 1551. The whole Bible divided into its present verses was first published in 1555. According to Stephanus's son, his father made the divisions into verses "*inter equitandum*" on a journey from Paris to Lyons. Although some have taken this to mean "on horseback" (and have explained occasional inappropriate verse divisions as originating when the horse bumped his pen), a better interpretation is that he accomplished the task at intervals while he rested at inns along the road.

The verse divisions devised by Stephanus were widely and rapidly adopted and first appeared in English in the Geneva Bible (New Testament, 1557; entire Bible, 1560). Despite its usefulness, however, the system has been criticized for two reasons. First, the divisions sometimes occur in the middle of a sentence, breaking the natural flow of thought. Second, to the reader, the broken text appears to be a series of separate and detached statements rather than a unit. It is too late to change the system to correct inappropriate verse divisions, so most Bible publishers try to make the text as continuous as possible, dividing it into logical paragraphs, printing the verse divisions in the margin or inconspicuously in the text. (In most editions of the King James Version each verse is printed as a separate paragraph.)

The Use of Italics

Aldus Manutius (1450–1515), a Venetian printer, startled Europe in 1501 by publishing the writings of Virgil in a new font of type, characterized by sloping letters that somewhat resembled handwriting. This new typeface was called *italic*. Over time, people realized that this new typeface was not easy to read. That is why italic type is not used today for the body of a document but is reserved for such things as the titles of books and magazines, foreign words and phrases, scientific names of genera and species, the names of plaintiff and defendant in legal citations, and, most commonly, to indicate special emphasis. None of these categories, unfortunately, accounts for the italics in certain versions of the Bible.

Bible publishers started using italics in the text of the Holy Scriptures in the sixteenth century. Publishers used italic type for words that are not translations of specific words in the original but were added by translators to complete or clarify the meaning of a word or phrase. The King James Version of 1612 followed this practice. The practice became standard in subsequent editions of the KJV and continues even now. This use of italics does have its problems. For example, in 1 Kings 13:27, the prophet Shemaiah says to his sons, "Saddle my ass." The verse then continues, "And they saddled *him*." In this case, the word supplied to round out the translation could refer either to the ass or to Shemaiah. It is not unambiguously clear.[1] The translation committee for the Revised Standard Version abandoned the practice of using italics for these additions because it felt that such words were an essential part of the translation and did not need to be highlighted. Other English versions of the Bible have also dropped the use of italics because publishers regard their use as misleading. Moreover, because italics are generally used to show special emphasis, publishers are afraid that people will assume that this is what they mean in the sacred text. I hope this primer on the "physical" dimensions of the Bible will help us better understand the biblical text.

How Can I Prepare for the Process of Academic Biblical Study?

It has been so long since I started my academic study of the Bible that I have all but forgotten what it is like to walk into a biblical studies class for the first time. So, I asked my students what would have been most helpful for them to know when they began academic biblical study. The insights and advice that follow are the result of our conversations and their essays.

1. Be prepared for a course that will focus on the text and not your personal appropriation of it. As I mentioned earlier, the aims of biblical scholarship are different from those of the garden-variety Bible study or Sunday school class. People take academic Bible courses for a number of different reasons, one of which is to strengthen their own faith. As one student said, "I think I began academic Bible

study . . . with the idea that by increasing my academic knowledge of religion, I would strengthen my faith." He then qualified this statement by saying, "An academic study of the Bible can be useful preparation for answering the doubts, questions, and preconceptions of religion that often come up, especially during college years, when religion debates seem to come up all the time in dorms, fraternities, etc. However, to think that reading the Bible as homework can somehow become one's daily devotional is ludicrous."

Attention to the text is of paramount importance in the classroom. In many ways, a Bible class is an exercise in deconstruction. In attempting to explain the text, the Bible course seeks to avoid, as much as possible, the question of how a particular interpretation can be integrated into your faith journey. Questions of integration are left up to the student. In response, some students become frustrated with a course, because they feel that their fundamental devotional and faith questions are not being answered. The student must keep in mind that a Bible course seeks to be like any other course in an academic environment; that is, it attempts to discuss the subject in as objective a manner as possible. As one student said, "No matter what your reason or motivation for taking a Bible class, you should always attempt to keep your religious and personal views of the text out of your study." Yes, your personal devotion to a religious community is an important part of who you are, but do not expect the academic study of the Bible to be a substitute for participation in a faith community.

2. Be prepared for an environment where the words "what I believe" can be a form of academic suicide. One of the reasons we study the Bible in an academic environment is that we find it meaningful for our personal and corporate existence. We come to a course with certain ideas about what the text means. Elders or other religious authorities have often handed down this meaning to us. However, personal belief

cannot serve as the *only* basis upon which to build an academic argument. Furthermore, you should be prepared to have your views challenged and questioned when they are expressed in an academic setting. This reality is often startling to students. They do not understand how their personal convictions can be questioned on the public stage. Yet this is the nature of the academic enterprise. As one student said, "If you can't back up what you think with anything but your own faith, it has no place in an academic argument or paper. Save it for church."

3. Be prepared for an environment where the professor and others may have their own agendas. Professors, like everyone else, have their own views on all kinds of subject matter. While professors should strive to be as objective as possible when analyzing the biblical material, this does not always happen. Just as a history professor may have his or her own views on the meaning of historical events, biblical scholars have theirs about faith issues. It is often as difficult for teachers as it is for students to separate their faith convictions from their academic pursuits. One student admitted that his new academic understanding of the Bible placed greater responsibility on him in his conversations with others than he had ever felt before: "I have found that it is often difficult to separate my academic convictions from my spiritual ones when leading a discussion or answering questions about scriptures that I have studied." Realizing that ideas and interpretations create reality for ourselves and others, he now understands the power of knowledge and the need to use that power responsibly: "Anyone who shares one's faith with others must be prepared to accept responsibility for those spoken words to others." The same is true for instructors. Although your instructor may have a personal agenda, when it comes to biblical study, it is your responsibility to engage the materials regardless of another's agenda.

4. Be prepared for an experience that may change your life. The consequences of this can be positive, negative, or both. If you are not prepared for what will transpire in the classroom, the negative consequences of biblical scholarship can cause you to become embittered about the discipline. Biblical scholarship can challenge accepted and traditional interpretations of biblical texts. In response, some students just "shut down" and refuse to engage biblical scholarship in a creative way at all. Other students engage the materials and learn the discipline, but understand biblical scholarship as a bitter pill to swallow. And while this is a better response to the presentation of biblical scholarship in the classroom, it is not the one most biblical scholars hope to elicit.

The final possible response to biblical scholarship—the one sought by biblical scholars—is that you find the academic study of the Bible to be a positive experience. In order to facilitate this positive response, I offer a comment made by one of the students: find a professor (or another Christian with an academic background) you know and trust, and don't hesitate to ask that professor questions. For biblical scholarship to be a positive experience, the encounter in the classroom should be complemented by an equally positive and understanding experience outside the classroom. In my own life, church activities and devotional life helped me integrate my classroom experience with my faith journey. I hope that these comments regarding preparation, and the rules of thumb in the chapters that follow, will contribute to making your experience of academic biblical scholarship a positive one.

2

Rules of Thumb for Reading and Interpreting Biblical Texts

A Basic Approach

RULE OF THUMB 1: When you read the Bible, approach it as you would any other book.

One of the hallmarks of modern biblical scholarship has been the groundbreaking idea that we should read the Bible as we would any other book or classic work—for example, Homer's *Iliad* or Thackeray's *Vanity Fair.* This means that we must take a *critical* attitude toward the text (see the discussion on "critical" on pages 4–5). Engage the text. Ask it questions. Seek to understand what it is trying to say. Unfortunately, people sometimes confuse being critical with being negative. Reading critically does not mean taking a negative attitude toward what we are studying. The purpose of biblical scholarship is not to undermine the Bible, but to uncover as much about the text as we possibly can. Uncovering the text means, in part, uncovering the origins of the text.

Sometimes, when we read the Bible, things do not make sense. At times, we may be inclined simply to overlook the incongruency. For example, Exodus 2:18 identifies the priest of Midian, Moses' father-in-law, as Reuel. However, Exodus 3:1—just eight verses later—identifies the priest of Midian as Jethro. Which name is correct? There are three obvious possibilities, each supported by some scholars: (1) The priest of Midian was addressed by both names. (2) The different names for the priest of Midian reflect two different narrative traditions, one calling the priest Reuel, the other calling him Jethro. (3) The two names for the priest of Midian reflect totally fictitious narrative traditions, that is, stories with no real basis in history. We might, though, decide that these inconsistencies do not matter. But it is the job of the interested reader to catch things like this and figure out what they mean.

Scholars try to explain the meaning of such inconsistencies in the most plausible manner possible. To some, the most reasonable way to understand what is going on in Exodus is option 2 above: Two separate stories—two narrative traditions—were joined together to form a single story, and this was done at some later time by a person not involved in the creation of either story. One of the common assumptions behind this position is that both stories have some basis in historical fact. Unfortunately, this is almost impossible to prove. There is just not sufficient evidence (e.g., archaeological findings, other written sources, indications at other points in the text) to prove beyond a reasonable doubt that either of these traditions originally derive from something that happened in history. However, history does not provide conclusive proof for our understanding the Bible. Rather, the point of the story is the deciding measure. And the point of the story may have little or nothing to do with history. In short, we must look at the peculiarities of a story in order to figure out its point, rather than look to history as the crucial measure of the Bible's truthfulness.

An astute reader must also be attentive to the changes that occur in the same or similar stories when they are told in different parts of the Bible. Take the resurrection accounts as an example. Mark's story is clearly different from Matthew's.

Markan Account (Mark 16:1–5)	*Matthean Account* (Matt. 28:1–5)
1 When the sabbath was over, Mary Magdalene, and Mary the mother of James, and Salome bought spices, so that they might go and anoint him.	1 After the sabbath, as the first day of the week was dawning, Mary Magdalene and the other Mary went to see the tomb.
2 And very early on the first day of the week, when the sun had risen, they went to the tomb.	2 And suddenly there was a great earthquake; for an angel of the Lord, descending from heaven, came and rolled back the stone and sat on it.
3 They had been saying to one another, "Who will roll away the stone for us from the entrance to the tomb?"	3 His appearance was like lightning, and his clothing white as snow.
4 When they looked up, they saw that the stone, which was very large, had already been rolled back.	4 For fear of him the guards shook and became like dead men.
5 As they entered the tomb, they saw a young man, dressed in a white robe, sitting on the right side; and they were alarmed.	5 But the angel said to the women, "Do not be afraid; I know that you are looking for Jesus who was crucified."

These differing accounts in some ways raise more questions than they solve. For example, how many women went to the tomb? Mark says three. Matthew says two. Was there an earthquake, or did the young man roll back the stone? Was there a young man, or was there an angel? Was this person (young man/angel) sitting in the tomb or on the stone outside the tomb? We must ask, how can these recount the same story when so many elements in the stories are different? There are no easy answers to these questions, and scholars must often be satisfied with saying that the accounts cannot be reconciled.

As a student of the text, your job is to notice such discrepancies and attempt to understand why they occur. You should not act as if the discrepancies are not there, because they are. We can *truly* understand what the text is trying to tell us only when we can accurately account for its problems, contradictions, and discrepancies. These "problem points" are where the real importance and meaning of the text is passed on. Again, as with the question about Moses' father-in-law, the student must be attentive to what the Bible itself is saying. The only way to do this properly is to grant no special privileges to the Bible that make it a book that can never be seriously questioned. (We grant special privileges to the Bible whenever we refuse to ask tough questions simply because it is the Bible.)

RULE OF THUMB 2: Be careful not to read your modern assumptions into ancient texts.

The Bible was written by many different people over a number of centuries. The most recent writings in the Bible go back at least eighteen hundred years. As twentieth-century people we have prejudices and assumptions that the people of the Bible knew nothing of. The ancients were very different from us. Take, for example, the ancient law of levirate marriage in the Hebrew Bible. The law reads:

> When brothers reside together, and one of them dies and has no son, the wife of the deceased shall not be married outside the family to a stranger. Her husband's brother shall go in to her, taking her in marriage, and performing the duty of a husband's brother to her, and the firstborn whom she bears shall succeed to the name of the deceased brother, so that his name may not be blotted out of Israel.(Deut. 25:5–6)

A brother must marry his dead brother's wife. Not just that, the living brother must impregnate his new wife so that she can have a son who will legally belong to his deceased brother. This seems outrageous to us, but it was the way things worked in ancient Israel. Our first encounter with this kind of marriage comes in Genesis 38, where Judah's son, Er, dies without a son. Judah instructs his next eldest son, Onan, to perform his duty to his deceased brother. As the Bible tells us, Onan was not happy with this arrangement: "[S]ince Onan knew that the offspring would not be his, he spilled his semen on the ground whenever he went in to his brother's wife, so that he would not give offspring to his brother" (Gen. 38:9). In response to Onan's disobedience, God strikes him dead.

Another example of a situation involving levirate marriage comes to us from the book of Ruth. In this story, because of famine, a family from Bethlehem journeys to Moab, a country bordering on Canaan. There the father Elimelech dies, and the two sons, Mahlon and Chilion, take Moabite wives, Ruth and Orpah. After ten years the sons die, leaving no offspring. Their mother Naomi is deprived of any way to support herself, since she has no (male) children. Hearing of food back in Canaan, she decides to return. When her daughters-in-law decide to accompany her on this journey, Naomi asks them to remain in Moab. Orpah consents to Naomi's request, but Ruth resolves to stay with Naomi. In Bethlehem the two women seek food. Ruth gleans in the fields of a wealthy man named Boaz, a relative of Elimelech. His kindness prompts Naomi to devise a plan for securing a home for Ruth. At Naomi's urging, Ruth goes to the threshing floor at night and asks Boaz to marry her. Although he is willing to marry Ruth, he must first determine if a closer relative to Elimelech wishes to assume responsibility for her. The unnamed relative refuses, and Boaz marries Ruth. She bears a son, Obed, who continues the family line and becomes the grandfather of King David.

Chapter 3 of Ruth is crucial to the story, since it deals with the legal questions of levirate marriage and the associated claim to land. The ancient world was very different from our world. Because women, children, slaves, and resident aliens were not considered full citizens or members of the community, they could not usually assert legal claims, especially claims to land. A poor widow like Ruth was in a desperate social situation if she could not remarry after the death of her husband.

The status of women in the Bible, like Ruth, highlights one of the profound differences between the ancient world and ours. The indignities committed against Hagar the Egyptian slave (Genesis 16), Dinah (Genesis 34), and the two Tamars (Genesis 38; 1 Kings 13) arise partly out of the dynamics of women's status in the family and society. A childless widow had little freedom and was supposed to return to her father's house (Lev. 22:13). Widows with sons, divorced women, and prostitutes were probably less dependent on male authority, but if they were poor, their lives could become precarious in the absence of a related male protector. Fortunately, in modern industrial societies like ours, fewer people are subject to such fickle fate. But do not assume that women, children, and others in the Bible had the same legal or human rights we value today. They were considered not people but something akin to property.

Things had changed considerably for women by the time of the writing of the New Testament, but attitudes toward women were still patriarchal and hierarchical. (Come to think of it, some of these attitudes still flourished just thirty years ago.) To a great extent, a woman's status depended on the family into which she was born, so it would be more precise to speak of the status of wealthy Roman women; wealthy women who were not Roman citizens; poor women, both Roman and non-Roman; and women slaves. However, we can make some general statements regarding the status of women.

In general, women were dependent both financially and legally on the men in their lives—fathers, husbands, uncles, brothers, and sons. Women generally married while still teenagers, bore one or more children, and died young, often in childbirth (the average life expectancy was thirty-four years). If a girl survived childhood, which could not be taken for granted, and as an adult survived childbirth, she might live a long life and bury her husband. In fact, women were the primary caretakers of the graves of family members, including those of in-laws. It was also women who passed on the household religious practices, such as ancestor worship, to their descendants.

We should not too quickly determine, however, that *all* women lived such lives of dependence. Wealthy women living in villas or in urban areas often functioned as chief household managers, especially when their husbands were absent for long periods of time. But while there were independent and wealthy women in the ancient world and a fortunate few who enjoyed "middle-class" stability, most women lived in slavery or near poverty. The majority worked for wages necessary for their own and their family's economic survival, even if they were married to a merchant or freedman. Some women may have been secluded in their homes, but for the most part they moved freely in many spheres of the Greco-Roman world.

Evidence from both Jewish and Greco-Roman documents shows, for example, that women held leadership roles in certain religious groups. In Judaism, archaeological and other evidence demonstrates that some women in the first few centuries C.E. held such positions as head of a synagogue, leader, elder, "mother of the synagogue," and priest. The exact functions of these women are difficult to determine, but their roles were probably equivalent to those of the men who bore parallel titles. The evidence further demonstrates that women were often integrated into regular services, not segregated in "women's galleries" or separate rooms, and that some were major financial contributors to local synagogues. Women also worked as midwives, lawyers, merchants, artists, teachers, physicians, prostitutes, laborers, and professionals of all sorts. And yet it was doubted in Jesus' day that women actually had what would come to be called a soul, and therefore women were not seen as candidates for salvation. Of course, this view of women has been amended (for example, women can be members of the religious community because they are in need of the same salvation as men), but the status of women is still debated in Christian circles today (for instance, some denominations debate whether women should be permitted to lead congregations as ministers). The problematic status of women in the ancient world explains why, although we know that women were among the early followers of Jesus, we hear so little about them.

One last example of the difference between us and ancient biblical people and society concerns a concept that was central to Jesus' teaching, the kingdom of God. Citizens of modern democracies may easily misinterpret what is meant by the term "kingdom" in Jesus' preaching and teaching. When the Bible speaks of kings and kingdoms, it does not mean constitutional monarchs like Queen Elizabeth II or the Emperor of Japan and the lands they rule. Rather, it is referring to a monarch whose will is supreme. There is no parliament in the New Testament concept of kingdom. When we read passages describing what the kingdom is like—or when we find people using kingdom language—we must keep in mind that they are talking about a social and political structure that is very different from our own.

RULE OF THUMB 3: The more you try to do, the less you'll really understand.

There is a general esthetic rule of thumb: Less is more. This rule of thumb also applies to reading the Bible. Cramming to read large chunks of the Bible often keeps us from reading the text carefully. Scholars, in contrast, usually concentrate on small tracts of text. We can learn from that practice and recognize that to understand the Bible, we generally must slow down our reading pace. It may become necessary to reread a passage to make sure that we understand what it is trying to communicate. *Depth* of understanding of a particular text is preferable to breadth or volume of reading. In other words, it is better to have a thorough understanding of a few verses than a cursory understanding of an entire book.

There is no way you can read the book of Genesis in an evening or two and do it justice. Genesis deals with the creation of the world, primeval history, a great flood, the dispersion of peoples throughout the earth, the patriarchs, and much more. It would be extremely difficult to digest and reflect on all this information in an evening. And for short texts, like the letter to Philemon, my advice is the same: *Be careful not to rush through the text.* The books of the Bible deal with profound ideas that are not always directly communicated to the reader. For example, is Paul ordering Philemon to free Onesimus, or is he doing something else, like flattering Philemon into releasing his slave? Is Onesimus really a slave? What about the rhetoric of the text? That is, why does Paul use such flowery language when addressing Philemon? Is this the way he would normally address Philemon, or is this his strategy to get Philemon to act the way he wants? To deal with these kinds of questions productively, we often need to reread a passage in order to understand better its meaning. So never rush through a reading. Take it slow, and interact with the text. (See Rule of Thumb 5 below for further discussion of this idea.)

RULE OF THUMB 4: A translation is only as good as its translator.

This should not come as a surprise, in light of the discussion on biblical languages in chapter 1, but it bears repeating: The Bible was not written in English. Neither Moses nor Jesus communicated with anyone in English. No, the Bible was written in Hebrew and Greek, except for those parts of the Jewish scriptures written in Aramaic. This means that whenever we read the Bible in English, we are reading a translation. Translations can be done by individuals or by groups, but they are all, to varying degrees, only the best estimates of what the author was trying to communicate.

Have you ever tried to translate something from one language to another? It is not always easy. Not all ideas move easily from one language to another. Take, for example, the New Testament term *charis*. *Charis* is not easily translatable into English. Often it means "grace," but it also means "gift." And since the concept of *charis* is more important than the exact term itself, the relationship between grace and gift is fundamental to understanding what the New Testament is trying to communicate. The context of a biblical passage is often helpful in determining what a term is supposed to mean, but not always. Even when translators can come up with an English word or words to convey what the Hebrew or Greek text is trying to express, the English often does not capture the full range of the term's meaning. It is a translation, and a translation is dependent upon the skill of the translator.

Most of the time we assume that one translation of the Bible is just as good as another. This is simply not true. When we read a translation, we are at the mercy of the abilities and prejudices of the translator. If the translator is skillful, then we may have a good translation, which means we have a good basis upon which to build an understanding of the text. If the translator is not skillful, then we may end up totally misunderstanding the text. People who do not read Hebrew or Greek may not be able to distinguish a good translation from a bad one. Unfortunately, sometimes the easiest translations to understand are the least accurate translations of the text, because the lack of precision means that the translator has tried to do our job for us, namely, to determine what the terms mean in the context of the passage.

How do we protect ourselves from a bad translation? There are a number of options.

1. Always use a Bible that has been translated by a committee of accredited scholars. This is no guarantee that the translators did not "drop the ball" at times, but if a Bible has been translated by a committee, then we probably are getting a less biased translation because negotiations took place. Furthermore, if the translators are from different faith communities or traditions, the translation will likely be less biased. Let the translators fight it out in a committee when it comes to how a translation should read!

2. Whenever possible, read more than one translation of a text. Use a "parallel Bible," that is, a Bible that lays out three or four translations of the same text side by side. Comparing the translations can give a reader more insight into the ideas the text is trying to relate.

3. Avoid translations that try to make the scriptures too idiomatic, that is, too informal, like the style of language we use with each other on a regular basis. Language changes, and fad Bibles go the way of fad clothes. It is important that the translations we read and compare are not overly constrained by the limitations of modern idiomatic English.

4. Whenever possible, consult critical commentaries, which help to make the text more accessible. Commentaries like the *International Critical Commentary* can give us more insight into the problems in translating a particular passage. Articles in these commentaries can assist the person who does not know biblical languages to understand the issues involved in translation. It is not as easy as

one might think to express in a modern, living language the meaning of a passage written in a once-living and ancient language.

A Short Note on English-Language Bible Translations

The King James Version

What about the King James Version (KJV)? Is it an acceptable translation? Well, yes and no. The KJV is many things. It is poetic, lyrical, and probably the noblest English translation of scripture ever accomplished. King James I of England commissioned it on February 10, 1604, because there were two competing English Bibles: the Bishops' Bible and the Geneva Bible. At a conference of theologians and church officials held in January of the same year, the call had been made for a new translation. James ordered that "a translation be made of the whole Bible, as consonant as can be to the original Hebrew and Greek, and this is to be set out and printed without any marginal notes and only to be used in all Churches of England in time of Divine Service." The committee was composed of fifty-four men, who worked in six companies, each of which was assigned a section of the Bible (three for the Hebrew Bible, two for the New Testament, and one for the Apocrypha). Seven years later, the committee published its work as the KJV. After its 1611 publication, the KJV rapidly went through several editions, nearly all of which had changes in the text. The edition of 1614, for instance, differed from the 1611 edition in over 400 places. Dr. Benjamin Blayney of Oxford (1769) made the most careful and comprehensive revision. It took approximately forty years before the 1611 edition of the KJV replaced the Geneva Bible in the people's hearts.

In 1870, the Church of England authorized another revision of the KJV. Americans were even invited to participate in the revision, but with the condition that the American edition not be published until fourteen years after the appearance of the British edition. All agree that the work was done carefully. In the New Testament alone about 30,000 changes were made, many on the basis of having found a better Greek text to use in the translating process.

The outstanding feature of the KJV is the sheer beauty of its language. The translators were all experienced in the public reading of the scriptures and in the conduct of public worship. When they chose the final wording of a passage, it was often determined by their instinct for what would sound "good" when read aloud.

The persistent problems with the KJV are twofold. First, the KJV (and the New KJV) are based primarily on an essentially flawed Greek text known as the *Textus Receptus*. Second, since the revision of the KJV in 1870 (published in 1881), a mountain of newly discovered papyri has changed scholars' opinions of how the text should be read. In short, we have better tools and resources to use when constructing a good translation of the Bible (see below). The KJV is good for personal study, and it sounds great in church, but it is a poor translation to use for any study of the Bible—it's a language not only outdated, but in some respects, arcane. So, even if you can go out and learn Greek and Hebrew, your best bet is to follow these rules of thumb and keep in mind that translation is not always easy.

Other English-Language Translations

Many Bibles—there have been more than 250 translations of the New Testament alone—have appeared since 1611. Robert Young, an Edinburgh bookseller who is most famous for his *Analytical Concordance to the Bible*, published his own literal translation in 1862. Charles Thomson, secretary of the Continental Congress, translated the Greek version of the Hebrew Bible and the New Testament and published it in 1808. Thomson was the first person to translate the Greek version of the Jewish Scriptures into

English and the first person to publish an English New Testament in America.

The modern era of English-language Bible translation began with the *Twentieth Century New Testament*, which appeared in its definitive form in 1904. The project was initiated by Mary Higgs, the wife of a Congregational minister, and Ernest Malan, a signal and telegraph engineer, both of whom were troubled by the fact that the language of the KJV was so difficult for young people to understand. One of their advisors was Richard Weymouth, a classical scholar, whose own *New Testament in Modern Speech* was published posthumously in 1902. Weymouth wanted to produce a translation that laypeople could understand and use for private reading, not public worship.

According to some scholars, the modern translation that had the greatest impression on the Bible-reading public was by the Scottish scholar James Moffatt. His translation of the New Testament, published in 1913, was titled *The New Testament: A New Translation*; his translation of the Hebrew Bible appeared in 1924; and the whole Bible was revised in 1935. Moffatt spent his last years as professor of church history at Union Theological Seminary in New York.

Edgar J. Goodspeed, of the University of Chicago, answered the long-felt need for a New Testament in American English. "For American readers . . . who have had to depend so long upon versions made in Great Britain," he said, "there is room for a New Testament free from expressions which . . . are strange to American ears." Goodspeed's *New Testament, An American Translation* was published in 1923. In 1927 a group of scholars led by J. M. Powis Smith produced a translation of the Hebrew Bible, which in 1935 was published with Goodspeed's New Testament as *The Bible, An American Translation*. In 1938 Goodspeed translated the Apocrypha, and *The Complete Bible: An American Translation* appeared in 1939.

In 1961, the Jehovah's Witnesses (Watch Tower Bible and Tract Society) published a translation of the Bible under the title *New World Translation of the Holy Scriptures,* which reflected the theological convictions of the Witnesses, most vividly displayed in John 1:1, "and the Word was a god." In 1972, the Watch Tower Bible and Tract Society published a posthumous translation by Steven Byington, mainly, it appears, because he used Jehovah as the proper name of God.

The Revised Standard Version (RSV) followed in the King James tradition, trying to translate the text literally. In 1937, the International Council of Religious Education had authorized a revision of the American edition of the 1881 KJV, stating that it should "embody the best results of modern scholarship as to the meaning of the scriptures, and express this meaning in English diction which is designed for use in public and private worship and preserves those qualities which have given to the King James Version a supreme place in English literature." The work was done by thirty scholars. The New Testament appeared in 1946, the Old Testament in 1952, and the Apocrypha in 1957. In 1977 an "Expanded Edition" appeared, which included not only the Roman Catholic deuterocanonical books (i.e., books in the Septuagint but not in the Hebrew canon. Protestants call them the Apocrypha.), but also 3 and 4 Maccabees and Psalm 151, thus making it acceptable to Eastern Orthodox churches.

The New Revised Standard Version (NRSV), published in 1990, is a paradigm of what a revision of an existing translation should be. In matters of text, exegesis, and language the NRSV is on its way to becoming the most widely used translation among mainline biblical scholars. It has dropped archaic terms and obsolete language. It has tackled the difficult task of making the English text inclusive where the original is intended to be inclusive. Some, however, have criticized the guiding principle of the committee—"as literal as possible, as free as necessary"—as producing a translation heavy on the literalism and light on the freedom.

And problems and disagreements persist. The RSV was received with mixed reviews. While its publication generated appreciation and gratitude in some circles, it was criticized and condemned, especially by conservative Protestants. Because of its sponsorship by the National Council of Churches, the RSV was seen by conservatives as tainted by liberal beliefs. It was even said that the translation committee included Communist sympathizers. Conservatives countered with translations of their own. These various translations were well received, but until the 1978 publication of the *New International Version* (NIV), none achieved the status of *the* Bible acceptable to a majority of conservative Protestants, most of whom were still using the KJV. The advertising campaign for the NIV focused on the trustworthiness of the translators themselves, who, it was claimed, had "a high view of Scripture," believing that the Bible, in its entirety, "is the Word of God written and is therefore inerrant in the autographs."

In sum, while the NRSV is now the standard version used by more theologically liberal academics, the KJV and NIV are the favored versions for those who view the NRSV with suspicion, including conservative academics. A glance at which Bibles are actually used in churches reveals that the KJV is still king. Part of the reason for its dominance may be economic; the KJV is a cheaper translation than most others because it is not subject to the copyright laws that make new translations more expensive. (One may also learn a great deal about the theological convictions of a particular congregation [or denomination] from its choice of translation for its pew Bibles.) For the most part, scholars have definite convictions as to what Bible they want used in a course, and it is prudent for a student to use that translation when taking the course.

RULE OF THUMB 5: When reading a text, don't ask and it won't tell.

We come to the scriptures with an idea that they have something important to tell us. Sometimes we ask our questions and get an answer, but at other times we may miss answers the Bible seeks to give, because we don't ask questions. What do I mean? Well, I am talking about our need to interact with the text in such a way that it provokes questions in us and we then seek to have the text answer those questions.

In the Hebrew Bible we come across passages that seem clear initially. But when we ask further questions about them, we have to begin to rethink old assumptions. A good example of this is the Ten Commandments (Ex. 20:1–17). Have you ever noticed that there are no punishments given for breaking the big ten? Compare this to other commandments like: "Whoever strikes a person mortally shall be put to death" (Ex. 21:12). Why aren't sanctions part of the Ten Commandments so we know the price for breaking them? Finding the answer to this question is part of the goal of interpretation. Does the text of Exodus give us a reason why there are no sanctions or penalties? Does the absence of punishment mean that the Ten Commandments were not meant to be taken as rules but as guidelines for action? Are punishments not given because the Ten Commandments are explained in the commandments that follow them? It is the task of the reader to ask these questions and attempt to determine the answer(s).

In the New Testament, many of my students skip over passages that appear self-explanatory. For example, they apply this "don't ask, don't tell" attitude toward reading the opening chapter of Matthew. Students often skip right past those first seventeen verses on genealogy and pick up the story at verse 18. Unfortunately, they miss the important concepts that are introduced in that section. They miss the unusual nature of the genealogy itself. Matthew 1:1 is odd because it names the genealogy according to its last entry (i.e., Jesus) rather than according to its first entry (i.e., Abraham). The astute reader should notice this and ask, Why? There is something else odd about this genealogy. In direct contrast to genealogies found in the Hebrew Bible, the Matthean genealogy names four women—Tamar, Rahab, Ruth, and the wife of Uriah—among the cast of characters that leads to Jesus. Again, the reader must ask, Why? There must be some reason for this. It does not seem reasonable to believe that Matthew created a genealogy that diverged so clearly from the Hebrew Bible pattern without some rationale. It is such interaction with the text that students are called upon to achieve when they study the Bible in an academic setting. (That is why Rule of Thumb 3 is there. When we read slowly, we ask more questions.)

RULE OF THUMB 6: All other things being equal, people today are not different from people 2,000 years ago.

Two points must be made here.

First, when reading the Bible, we must approach the people in the text as if they were a lot like people today. Of course, there are social, political, and historical differences between ancients and moderns, but they were no less Homo sapiens than we are. Not enough time has passed for significant evolutionary changes. (If we are looking for evolutionary changes, we need far more time than a few thousand years.) Although the Bible deals with the beginning of recorded history, the people described in the Bible appear to be as intellectually reflective as we are. The writings of Julius Caesar, Cicero, Plato, and the like are powerful for us today at least partly because they struggle with the same life issues that we do in the twenty-first century. Similarly, Cain and Abel confronted the issue of sibling rivalry. Jacob had to deal with scheming in-laws. Jeremiah wrestled with credibility issues. Mary faced an unplanned pregnancy. Paul was a struggling pastor/evangelist. King Herod had to cope with feelings of inadequacy and integrity. If we could magically transport some of the biblical characters into the modern world, it would be clear that there is little difference between them and us. We look the same. We have approximately the same mental capacity. We may be taller, on average, but the basics are the same. So when we read the text, we should keep in mind that evolution has not transformed us that much.

Second, ancient connections to God are similar to modern connections to God. We seem to forget this sometimes. We routinely make the assumption that biblical characters were in some special relationship with God. We think that God's talking to Abraham was more real than God's talking to us. We may believe that at some special time in the past God actually spoke to people, while God talks to us only in indirect ways.

This is a curious problem for people studying the Bible, because the Bible itself says in Deuteronomy 34:10 that "never since has there arisen a prophet in Israel like Moses, whom the Lord knew face to face." The key question in this text is the meaning of the phrase "face to face." It suggests that God and Moses had a special relationship. This may have been so, but we cannot prove it. Furthermore, the relationship between Moses and God is described in the Bible itself as something special, unlike any other human relationship with God in the Hebrew Bible. Most scholars believe that the Bible makes such a statement about Moses in order to accentuate his position as the great lawgiver. At any rate, the clear meaning of the passage is that God speaks to others differently from how God speaks to Moses. As the book of Numbers makes clear, "Where there are prophets among you, I the LORD make myself known to them in visions; I speak to them in dreams. Not so with my servant Moses; he is entrusted with all my house. With him I speak face to face—clearly, not in riddles; and he beholds the form of the LORD" (Num. 12:6–8). This makes the statement from Deuteronomy understandable, although such a special relationship may not be historically verifiable. In cases such as these, where one cannot prove or disprove a claim, the claim itself must be considered irrelevant for the purposes of argument.

When we view the people in the Bible as being like ourselves, we are able to understand their mishaps and fortunes better. People in the Bible struggled with the realities of their world, just as we do. They struggled to hear God's "voice" in the midst of their circumstances, just as we do. They sometimes mistakenly attributed to God their own prejudices and misconceptions of the world, just as we do. We read their stories and analyze their experiences because, in spite of their human limitations, many believe that they found God in the midst of their circumstances, and we endeavor to understand the mechanics of that experience.

RULE OF THUMB 7: An overactive imagination can get you into trouble.

When we read the Bible, far too often we imagine the scene in a way that does not truly reflect physical reality. On the surface, there is nothing wrong with this practice. In fact, the successful communication of a narrative requires that readers are able to form some sort of mental image. We all do this when we read a good novel, for instance. A problem arises, however, when we allow our imaginations to get the best of us. If we imagine something to be the way it is not, we tamper with the truth.

Take the story of Jesus stilling the storm on the Sea of Galilee. We imagine how this would look. In Mark 4:35–41 we read the following:

> On that day, when evening had come, he said to them, "Let us go across to the other side." And leaving the crowd behind, they took him with them in the boat, just as he was. Other boats were with him. A great gale arose, and the waves beat into the boat, so that the boat was already being swamped. But he was in the stern, asleep on the cushion; and they woke him up and said to him, "Teacher, do you not care that we are perishing?" He woke up and rebuked the wind, and said to the sea, "Peace! Be still!" Then the wind ceased, and there was a dead calm. He said to them, "Why are you afraid? Have you still no faith?" And they were filled with great awe and said to one another, "Who then is this, that even the wind and the sea obey him?"

In almost all versions of this story, the body of water they are traveling on is called a sea—the Sea of Galilee. Americans, at least, tend to think of seas as large bodies of water, larger than lakes but smaller than oceans. The Great Lakes are a collection of lakes that are larger than we would normally think of when we picture lakes in our minds. When I lived in Chicago, I lived on the shore of Lake Michigan, one of the Great Lakes. You cannot see the other shore of Lake Michigan from the Chicago side. Lake Michigan is larger—greater—than your average lake. Well, the Sea of Galilee is much smaller than Lake Michigan.

I found this out when I visited Israel for the first time, and it gave me a whole new perspective on this story. A good swimmer could swim across the Sea of Galilee in a few hours. (The Sea of Galilee is not a sea at all; it is not even a great lake! It is really an average-size lake, the size of which has been magnified in the minds of those who live in a country where it rains so little. And we have magnified it in our own minds, assuming we know what "sea" means. We tend to read the words "Sea of Galilee" and think of some huge body of water, but that is not the case. Our overactive imaginations and our perceptions of what words like "lake" and "sea" mean distort the image in our minds.

RULE OF THUMB 8: Get a map.

A lot of places are named in the Bible: Bethel. Shechem. Jerusalem. Emmaus. Many times we read these place names but we have little or no idea where they are geographically in relationship either to each other or to the rest of the world. Sometimes locating a place on the map is not important, but, more often than not, it is helpful to the student of the Bible to consult a map when reading about places and itineraries in the scriptures.

Why is it so helpful? Take, for example, the story of Joseph and his brothers (Genesis 37ff.). We are not told initially where Jacob and his family reside, except in the land of Canaan. The first location named is Shechem (37:12), near which, we are told, Joseph's brothers were pasturing the flocks. We then are given the location of Jacob and Joseph, the valley of Hebron (37:14). When Joseph goes searching for his brothers, he is told that they have departed from the Shechem area and are now at a place called Dothan (37:17). A glance at a map will tell us that Shechem is located between Mt. Gerizim and Mt. Ebal, close to a tributary of the Jordan River. Jacob and Joseph are to the south of Shechem in a valley close to Hebron, near the Dead Sea. Dothan is northwest of Shechem in the hill country of Israel. The distance between the valley of Hebron and Dothan is about a hundred miles. Walking such a distance would have taken Joseph some time. We might not imagine this distance when we read that passage, so having a map available is helpful to the study of the Bible.

We also need a map when we begin reading the New Testament. In fact, the information on a map can give us additional *clues* or insight into the region under discussion. For example, the New Testament tells us that Jesus was raised in a place called Nazareth. Examining a map shows us that Nazareth is located on a hill in the northern region of Canaan known as the Galilee. We can also see that Nazareth (a small village) was about three miles east of Sepphoris.

Sepphoris was a major Greco-Roman city that flourished during the time of Jesus' life and ministry. We are told that Jesus' father was a carpenter (Matt. 13:55), but that designation may be a little misleading, for the Greek term used here can also be used to describe a laborer. It appears highly probable that Jesus' father, known as Joseph, worked in and around Sepphoris during the economic boom experienced in the region during the first century.

What does this mean? It means that Jesus would have had easy access to his non-Jewish neighbors and could have learned Greek and Latin. This possibility changes our understanding of the Gospels. It casts doubt over the idea that Jesus was an ignorant peasant Jew from an insignificant village in a backward and isolated part of the Roman Empire. No. By living (and possibly working) so close to Greeks and Romans—as well as to such a major city as Sepphoris—Jesus may have been more cosmopolitan than we had imagined. This may explain the lack of references to translators in passages where Jesus converses with people who speak Greek (e.g., the Syrophoenician woman) and/or Latin (e.g., Pontius Pilate) but probably not Aramaic. It is amazing what we can deduce from knowing some history and looking at a map!

RULE OF THUMB 9: Don't stereotype people without a really good reason.

People have a tendency when they read the Bible to look at its characters as representatives of attitudes or personality types and not as individuals. Now, sometimes this approach is valid. For example, when the Bible is discussing groups of people, they tend to be caricatured or stereotyped in a manner that is often not flattering. We are told nothing good about the Philistines and the Hittites. Likewise, in the New Testament the impression given of the Pharisees (and sometimes the Jews generally) is unflattering, particularly when it portrays them as blind adherents to the Mosaic law.

We should be careful not to confuse certain memories of events held by particular groups—or rhetorical flourishes on the part of the author—with an unbiased historical account of those events. The astute reader must evaluate the writer's perspective toward the group or the event. Does the writer have an "ax to grind" against the group? Is the portrayal of the person or group of people confirmed by other sources not found in the Bible? Does the author have anything to gain by portraying this person (or these people) in that manner? These questions must be answered before a proper interpretation of the passage can take place.

We can also idealize characters in such a way that we miss the point of a passage. It is not just that when we read the Bible we tend to cast certain people or groups as the villain(s); we can also misinterpret a passage because we overlook clear character problems with "good" people in that passage. Sometimes we support too completely the idea of a person's goodness, so that the person or group is no longer human but becomes representative of types of behavior or attitudes we should imitate. For example, most modern readers stereotype the patriarch Abraham as a great man of faith (or the father of faith) so that when recounting the Abraham story, they tend to practice the art of selective memory and overlook or dismiss passages that suggest he had character flaws.

Many people overlook or attempt to explain away Genesis 12:13, where Abraham tells Sarah to lie and say that she is his sister instead of his wife. We forget that Abraham grew exceedingly wealthy because of this act of deception. We stress texts like Genesis 15:6 "And [Abraham] believed the LORD; and the LORD reckoned it to him as righteousness" while overlooking passages like Genesis 16, the birth of Ishmael, and Genesis 17:17–18, where it reads, "Then Abraham fell on his face and laughed, and said to himself, 'Can a child be born to a man who is a hundred years old? Can Sarah, who is ninety-nine years old, bear a child?' And Abraham said to God, 'O that Ishmael might live in your sight!'" In other words, we selectively tell the story of Abraham in order to retain our preconception of the man, instead of seeing him in a more realistic and human manner. To me, what makes Abraham remarkable is that he was so flawed and still achieved so much for God, not that he is an exemplar of unquestioning obedience. The same is true for almost everyone else in the Bible. While we would like to remember only their grand moments, the reality is that real human beings struggle because they are a mixture of good and bad. This is what gives power to the story.

The same is true of the way we read the New Testament. One of the most serious mistakes we make in reading the New Testament is to believe that Jesus was never wrong. Generally, this attitude is grounded in the idea that Jesus is the hero of the Gospels and, therefore, the Gospel writers would never portray him as misunderstanding or acting improperly. Yet we have such evidence as Mark 7:24–30, in which Jesus initially refused to heal the daughter of a Syrophoenician woman because she was a Gentile. The woman responded to Jesus in such a manner that he changed his mind and granted her request. In other words, Jesus acknowledged that when he rejected the woman's request he made a mistake. This passage can teach us a lot about the problems of religious and ethnic pride, but it will teach us nothing if we attempt to explain away or rationalize the fact that Jesus (1) admitted that he had been incorrect, and (2) changed his mind. Likewise, we are hard-pressed to deal with passages like Mark 11:13–14, which cast doubt on the idea of Jesus' infallibility.

We cannot assume to know, absolutely, the character of persons in the Bible. We cannot allow ourselves to read them as stereotypes of "hero" and "villain" unless there is a good reason, based on the text, to do that. Furthermore, because biblical authors often stereotyped people, we should not assume their stories are unbiased historical fact. An astute reader must develop the skills necessary to differentiate between bias and objectivity in a presentation, because the meaning of the text rests in the balance!

RULE OF THUMB 10: The Bible means what it says, and says what it means. Except when it doesn't.

To make life simple, let us divide statements in the Bible into two groups: statements that are meant to be taken literally and those that are not. Literal statements are meant to be taken at face value. Nonliteral statements have a meaning that must be deduced or interpreted from the passage. This sounds simple enough, but distinguishing between the two types of statements can be difficult when reading the Bible. Sometimes we mistakenly take statements literally when they should be read as metaphors or taken nonliterally. And vice versa. How do we avoid making a mistake? Think of the context. It is the reader's job to decipher from the context in which it is placed what the text is trying to communicate. For example, a statement made in the Sermon on the Mount, like "In everything do to others as you would have them do to you" (Matt. 7:12a), probably should be understood differently from a statement made in a parable, like "Go and do likewise" (Luke 10:37), found in the parable of the Good Samaritan. The contexts of the statements are different. One is found in a sermon while the other is found in a parable, and that should be taken into account when we attempt to interpret them.

In the Hebrew Bible one of the most interesting passages is found in Ezekiel 1:15–21. The passage reads as follows:

> As I looked at the living creatures, I saw a wheel on the earth beside the living creatures, one for each of the four of them. As for the appearance of the wheels and their construction: their appearance was like the gleaming of beryl; and the four had the same form, their construction being something like a wheel within a wheel. When they moved, they moved in any of the four directions without veering as they moved. Their rims were tall and awesome, for the rims of all four were full of eyes all round. When the living creatures moved, the wheels moved beside them; and when the living creatures rose from the earth, the wheels rose. Wherever the spirit would go, they went, and the wheels rose along with them; for the spirit of the living creatures was in the wheels. When they moved, the others moved; when they stopped, the others stopped; and when they rose from the earth, the wheels rose along with them; for the spirit of the living creatures was in the wheels.

For hundreds of years people have wondered about the meaning of this passage. The image of this "wheel within a wheel" is hard to imagine. Is the entire image to be taken literally? Is *any* of this vision to be taken literally? What about these "living creatures"? How are they to be understood? Is this vision descriptive, or is it a metaphor for something else? The answer is not clear. Understanding this passage calls us to use all of our analytic and imaginative skills. The Bible does not supply us with clear-cut guidelines when it comes to interpreting visions like this one in Ezekiel, and so we remain uncertain as to how the vision should be interpreted.

Other passages in scripture are not as imaginative or "cosmic" as the one from Ezekiel, but they are no less perplexing. For example, in the Sermon on the Mount Jesus says something presumably straightforward: "If your right eye causes you to sin, tear it out and throw it away; it is better for you to lose one of your members than for your whole body to be thrown into hell. And if your right hand causes you to sin, cut it off and throw it away; it is better for you to lose one of your members than for your whole body to go into hell" (Matthew 5:29–30).

Does Jesus mean this to be taken literally? If so, why are there not more blind and lame people in churches today? If Jesus does not mean for us to take this statement literally, then how are we supposed to understand it? How can we make ourselves blind or lame without really being blind or lame? When Jesus says "eye" or "hand," does he mean some sort of idea or activity that "eye" or "hand" is supposed to represent? The answers are not clear. It is the reader's job to interpret the passage in a way that respects the text that comes before and after it, but also helps to explain it in a way that makes sense.

An interesting historical legend involves the third-century theologian and biblical scholar Origen of Alexandria. Origen read what Jesus said in Matthew 19:12: "For there are eunuchs who have been so from birth, and there are eunuchs who have been made eunuchs by others, and there are eunuchs who have made themselves eunuchs for the sake of the kingdom of heaven. Let anyone accept this who can." Origen, it is said, read this verse and understood Jesus to be speaking literally. So, in accordance with the phrase about those who make themselves eunuchs for the sake of the kingdom, Origen castrated himself in order to give himself totally to the Lord.

Ironically, Origen is known as one of the greatest allegorists, or nonliteralists, in Christian history. There was little that Origen read in the Bible that he thought should be taken literally, but, if this oft-repeated story is true, he believed that this was one of those passages. Most of us would not want to take that statement literally. Our question would likely be, Why? Why is it that we take some statements literally and others nonliterally? Could it be that our interpretation of a text is based on our prejudices—our likes and dislikes—more than on what the text itself says?

In other words, we must be careful when reading the Bible not to assume too quickly that we know what a passage means simply because we like to understand it that way. The astute reader must always be interacting with the text—asking questions of it—because through this interaction the Bible opens up new worlds of meaning for us.

The Advanced Approach

RULE OF THUMB 11: Don't ask Jon to tell you what Suzy meant.

An old real estate adage says, "The three most important things are *location, location, location*." One could give a similar adage for understanding the Bible: The three most important things in interpreting a biblical passage are *context, context, context*. What do I mean? One of the keys to understanding a biblical passage has to do with its placement. The biggest mistake an astute reader can make is to overlook the context and/or placement of a passage.

One of our goals when reading the Bible is to understand *how* we should interpret a particular verse or verses. The first step to getting at the meaning of a passage is to attempt to place the verse or verses within their particular context. When we look at and attempt to determine the context of a passage, we go a long way toward understanding what the passage is trying to tell us. Scholars call determining the context of a passage, discovering its "setting in life." (Theological scholars use the German phrase *Sitz im Leben*.)

A good example of the importance of context comes from my own experience, in fact, from my dissertation. I wrote my dissertation on the Lord's Prayer and how two intellectuals in the early church interpreted it. One of the first things I had to do was determine the exact context of the Lord's Prayer. At first glance this may seem like an easy task, but it is actually more complex than it may appear.

As scholars can best determine, the Lord's Prayer has existed in at least three forms since it was first used by the church. Two of these versions—called "recensions" by scholars—are in the New Testament Gospels of Matthew and Luke. The third version can be found in an early Christian work known as *The Teaching of the Twelve Apostles*, usually called just the *Didache* ("teaching") by scholars. Similarities and differences exist among the versions, but this is not the point of our discussion here.

What is important for us is that although there are differences among the three versions, they all appear in the same context. They all appear in places where they are used to teach the proper way to worship God. For example, Luke 11:1 says, "[Jesus] was praying in a certain place, and after he had finished, one of his disciples said to him, 'Lord, *teach* us to pray, as John *taught* his disciples'" (*emphasis mine*). Likewise, in the *Didache*, we get the statement, "And do not pray as the wicked [do]; pray instead this way, as the Lord directed in his gospel" (*Did.* 8:2). Finally, Matthew 6:9 says, "Pray then in this way."

In order to understand what the Lord's Prayer is trying to tell us, we must try to understand why the writer(s) of that particular piece of scripture chose to put it where it is. For example, in the Gospel of Matthew the Lord's Prayer is part of a "sermon" delivered by Jesus. But it is not included in the so-called Sermon on the Plain in the Gospel of Luke—a sermon somewhat parallel to the Sermon on the Mount. Why?

The reason has to do with the varying contexts in which the prayer is placed. In the Sermon on the Mount the

Lord's Prayer appears in a discussion that begins, "Beware of [or: Be on your guard in] practicing your piety before others" (Matt. 6:1). This tells us that what is coming next has to do with the proper way(s) to practice your piety. This is its *context*. Moreover, this section on "practicing your piety" appears in the *context* of a sermon designed to teach people how to be good disciples (see Matt. 5:2). Further, this sermon appears within the context of a Gospel that is designed to portray Jesus as a Jewish teacher.

In Luke's Sermon on the Plain, things are different. First, Jesus enters a crowd of people who were there "to hear him and to be healed of their diseases" (6:18). This is almost a mob scene, with people of all kinds jostling each other, trying to touch Jesus: "And all in the crowd were trying to touch him, for power came out from him and healed all of them" (6:19). In short, the "setting in life" in Luke is very different from the orderly scene in Matthew. In Luke people appear more concerned with being healed than being taught. Second, this sermon is much less "spiritual" than the one given in Matthew. The Sermon on the Plain blesses the "poor" with the kingdom of God instead of the Sermon on the Mount's "poor in spirit." It blesses those who are "hungry" instead of those who "hunger and thirst for righteousness." In other words, the Sermon on the Plain is not concerned with the question of being a good disciple and practicing your piety *in the same way* as the Sermon on the Mount. Thus, the Lord's Prayer would have been inappropriate in the Sermon on the Plain. The writer of Luke had to find another place to put it, a place that better fit the character of the prayer.

Luke, therefore, places the Lord's Prayer at the beginning of a transitional scene in the Gospel. We are told nothing regarding the location—or the other concrete facts of the situation—other than that an anonymous disciple asked Jesus to instruct them in the practice of prayer. This scene is very different from the one in Matthew. And while the basic "setting in life" may be the same—Jesus is teaching about the proper worship practices of a disciple—the context in other ways is quite different. Luke does not place the prayer in the midst of a sermon designed to instruct disciples. Luke does not place the prayer in the midst of a Gospel designed to portray Jesus as a great Jewish teacher. Teaching is important in Luke, but it is done, generally, through the medium of parables. Luke's Gospel does not have the same aim as Matthew's. Thus Luke's purpose for using the Lord's Prayer is different from Matthew's; so one of the keys to understanding the meaning of the text in Luke is a serious look at the context in which the Lord's Prayer was placed.

Cross-Referencing

Not understanding the importance of the context of a passage may lead to the sometimes fatal mistake of cross-referencing. Cross-referencing is the act of attempting to understand one biblical text by noting the presence of the same term, concept, doctrine, or idea in another biblical text, and then using that second biblical text as a means of interpreting the first. I was once in a group studying this story from the Gospel of Matthew:

> When they came to the crowd, a man came to him, knelt before him, and said, "Lord, have mercy on my son, for he is an epileptic and he suffers terribly; he often falls into the fire and often in the water. And I brought him to your disciples, but they could not cure him." Jesus answered, "You faithless and perverse generation, how much longer must I be with you? How much longer must I put up with you? Bring him here to me." And Jesus rebuked the demon, and it came out of him, and the boy was cured instantly. Then the disciples came to Jesus privately and said, "Why could we not cast it out?" He said to them, "Because of your little faith. For truly I tell you, if you have faith the size of a mustard seed, you will say to this

mountain, 'Move from here to there,' and it will move; and nothing will be impossible for you." (Matt. 17:14–20)

As the discussion of the passage progressed, someone asked, "What does Jesus mean here by faith?" Another individual, quoting Hebrews 11:1, said, "Now faith is the assurance of things hoped for, the conviction of things not seen." I was a little disturbed by this response, for the meaning of the term "faith" in Matthew is not identical to its meaning in Hebrews. In Matthew, "faith" has something to do with the disciples' trust in God's ongoing power to heal during the eventual absence of Jesus. In contrast, faith as used in Hebrews 11:1 has to do with the disciples' trust in God's promise to bring about the kingdom and their very important need to obey the dictates of the gospel. So, while the meanings of faith in these passages may be similar, they are not the same.

The problem with cross-referencing is twofold. First, it makes the intellectual mistake of presuming that an author does not explain what he means when he says what he says. To express this another way, when Paul talks about faith, he will explain what he means when he uses the word. There is no need for us to go to the Gospel of Mark to clarify what Paul means by faith. Likewise, when reading a story—as we saw with the resurrection stories—it does not do much good to try to use one story to explain another, because each author has a (slightly) different understanding of what the story means, and a story's particular meaning can be lost when it is homogenized with others. Seek to understand a story on its own merits. If you can't get away from the habit of comparing stories, compare them with the purpose of understanding and appreciating how each author relates the story, and with a keen awareness of the differences. The astute reader seeks to understand a work (a Gospel or a letter, for example) based on its own stated intentions and meanings and not on the basis of another work's intentions and meanings.

This is the only way to truly listen to the voice of an author (like the writer of Matthew) without hearing it through the voice of another author (like the writer of Hebrews).

Second, cross-referencing makes the historical mistake of assuming that the authors of the Bible had access to each other's works. By and large, this was not true. Matthew did not have Paul's writings in front of him when he wrote his Gospel, at least as best we can tell. Furthermore, the early church did not have the New Testament in the same form we do for at least a few hundred years after Jesus' ministry. The sixty-six-plus books of the Bible that we possess today did not exist as one collection almost two thousand years ago. The average church in the first century *may* have owned a copy of one Gospel or a couple of Paul's letters. Almost no church had the Hebrew Bible, and those few churches that did have the Jewish Scriptures almost always had it in its Greek version, known as the Septuagint. By contrast, today's translation of the Jewish Scriptures is based primarily on the Hebrew text. And those little cross-references that some Bibles have did not exist for the Bible's ancient readers, so they understood Genesis 15:6, when it talked about Abraham's faith, on the basis of what Genesis said about Abraham, and not on the basis of Hebrews 11:1. (Of course, there are exceptions, and sometimes intellectuals who had access to more than one document compared them, but these incidents were rare.)

Even when biblical authors may have had access to other writings, they did not consider those other writings too sacred to change. For example, Matthew appears to have had access to Mark. But while more than 90 percent of the information found in Mark appears in Matthew, Matthew frequently takes Mark's story and expands upon it. In other places, Matthew edits parts of Mark that he finds difficult to understand. A good example of this occurs in Mark 14:51–52. In his account of Jesus' arrest we get this odd statement: "A certain young man was following [Jesus], wearing nothing but a linen cloth. [The people arresting Jesus] caught hold of him, but he left the linen cloth and ran off naked."

Due to its highly suggestive nature (i.e., it implies an improper relationship between Jesus and the young man), Matthew edits this incident out when he tells the arrest story. This editing may make sense for Matthew, but it ruins the story Mark was telling, because, I believe, the same young man appears at the empty tomb dressed in a white robe (the traditional symbol of Christian baptism) and announces Jesus' resurrection. Mark uses the young man as a symbol of Christian discipleship. After his editing, Matthew makes a different point by having the women greeted by an angel. If you want to understand the Gospel of Mark, you must find the answers to your questions in Mark itself. Asking Matthew to tell you what Mark means may appear to be helpful at first, but only Mark can really explain Mark. The same is true in everyday life. If I did not understand what Jon meant when he made a statement, isn't it better for me to ask Jon than to ask Suzy?

RULE OF THUMB 12: If somebody in the Bible is upset about something, it's because someone else is doing it.

This idea is as true in the Bible as it is in our everyday lives. If there were no people stealing, there would be no reason to have a law against it. The reality is, however, that some people steal, and in response society has fashioned laws against stealing. Another example of this is the problem of crack cocaine. When I was growing up, there apparently was no such thing as crack cocaine. (Or, if it existed, neither I nor many of my contemporaries knew about it.) However, as I got older, crack cocaine became a problem in certain communities in the United States. In response to what some called an epidemic, legislators began to enact laws specifically against the use of crack cocaine. The same is true in the Bible.

The prophet Amos rails against his fellow Israelites because they practice social injustice, saying, "[T]hey sell the righteous for silver, and the needy for a pair of sandals— they who trample the head of the poor into the dust of the earth, and push the afflicted out of the way" (Amos 2:6–7). Here, Amos is saying that some Israelites were prospering at the expense of the poor. Israel was prosperous, but not all Israelites were benefiting from the economic boom. To use a modern phrase, the rich got richer while the poor got poorer. This situation gave rise to one of the most profound statements of the Bible: "But let justice roll down like waters, and righteousness like an everflowing stream" (5:24). Amos responded to the evils of his day by calling upon the logic of the Torah (the first five books of the Bible, particularly the laws laid down in the covenant of Sinai).

Likewise, in the New Testament people discuss rules of conduct that reflect problems that they perceive in society. In Matthew we find such a situation regarding divorce.

> Some Pharisees came to [Jesus], and to test him they asked, "Is it lawful for a man to divorce his wife for any cause?" He answered, "Have you not read that the one who made them at the beginning 'made them male and female,' and said, 'For this reason a man shall leave his father and mother and be joined to his wife, and the two shall become one flesh'? So they are no longer two, but one flesh. Therefore what God has joined together, let no one separate." They said to him, "Why then did Moses command us to give a certificate of dismissal and to divorce her?" He said to them, "It was because you were so hard-hearted that Moses allowed you to divorce your wives, but at the beginning it was not so. And I say to you, whoever divorces his wife, except for unchastity, and marries another commits adultery." (Matt. 19:3–9)

According to the practice at the time, reflected in the question posed by the Pharisees, a man could divorce his wife when he felt that it was necessary. Other evidence tells us that in the time of Jesus men often divorced their wives because they were barren. The logic behind this was that the promise of God to Abraham was to have numerous offspring, and if a woman was incapable of bearing children, she was incapable of helping her husband fulfill the Abrahamic promise. Thus, it was a religious duty of sorts for a man to divorce his wife and marry a woman who was capable of bearing children.

Jesus' response tells us that there is some doubt about this practice in the growing Christian community. The Christian argument against divorce rests on a particular understanding of the purpose of marriage. Marriage is not solely for the sake of having children; that is, it is not primarily about fulfilling the Abrahamic promise. Marriage, Jesus says, is about the human unity that God intended from the beginning of creation. "For this reason a man shall leave his father and mother and be joined to his wife, and the two shall become one flesh" (Matt. 19:5; Gen. 2:24). Notice that Jesus overlooks God's command to the couple to be "fruitful and multiply, and fill the earth" (Gen. 1:28). Instead he says that such unions are determined by God—whether the couple bears children or not—and human beings should not attempt to undermine them in any way. Faithfulness to the Abrahamic promise does not supersede faithfulness to God's purpose in creation.

The Pharisees then raise the issue of divorce against Jesus' understanding of God's purpose in creation. The Pharisees (representing the current social practice) ask, "Why then did Moses command us to give a certificate of dismissal and to divorce her?" (Matt. 19:7). That is, if God did not intend for human beings to practice divorce, then why was it permitted under the laws God gave us through Moses at Mount Sinai? Jesus responds to their question by saying that such legislation was allowed under the Mosaic covenant *not* because God recognized divorce as an acceptable state of human affairs, but because human beings were determined to make divorce an acceptable state of human affairs. Again, the argument is based on a particular understanding of God's purpose in creation. This logic allows Jesus to say that it may be true that divorce is the current state of affairs, "but at the beginning it was not so" (Matt. 19:8b). According to Jesus, the only grounds upon which one can claim to need a certificate of divorce is when unchastity is involved. In effect, he has stiffened the law in order to curb perceived abuses in the society.

Jesus' comments astonish the disciples, who respond by saying, "If such is the case of a man with his wife, it is better not to marry" (Matt. 19:10). People reading this passage often overlook this response. They seem to want to separate the two sentiments, perhaps because Jesus' response to their statement appears to be a negative assessment of marriage. He says, "Not everyone can accept this teaching, but only those to whom it is given" (Matt. 19:11). In this exchange Jesus has (and the early Christians have) undermined the Jewish idea that marriage is for the purpose of having children. In fact, Jesus has undermined the idea that marriage is necessary at all. This is what the discussion of eunuchs is all about in 19:12. In sum, this passage in Matthew gives us insight into one of the controversies that gripped the early church. Apparently, some people felt that abandoning singleness for marriage was in some way desiring a lesser state in life—a life devoted to family instead of God. This life is only further complicated when the question of procreation is added into the picture. So the prohibition against divorce and the subsequent counsel to live in a state of life that allows one to be totally dedicated to God arise because some are upset that people are choosing marriage and family over their dedication to God.

These rules do not arise because somebody is doing something right. Rather, they arise because it is determined that somebody is doing something wrong.

RULE OF THUMB 13: Everybody has skeletons in the closet.

We know this principle to be true in *our* lives, and it is no less true when it comes to people in the Bible. When you look at the characters in the Bible, you find that all of them have not only their shining moments but their questionable moments also. To be sure, most of us would like to be remembered for our great accomplishments, our noble deeds; and this is no less true for people in the Bible. Moreover, *we* prefer to remember their high moments instead of their low ones. Still, this kind of selective memory not only undermines the integrity of the biblical text; it also undermines the worth and meaning of its characters as human beings. If we remember only the highlights of people's careers, we in reality devalue the significance of the good that they did.

A good example comes from a story told by the Rev. Peter Gomes:

> In a debate in the Israeli Parliament in December 1995, Foreign Minister Shimon Peres said that he disapproved of some of the practices of King David, particularly of his conquest of other peoples, and his seduction of a married woman, Bathsheba, whose husband, Uriah the Hittite, David sent to his death. In I Kings 15:5, it is written that David "did what was right in the sight of Yahweh and did not turn aside from anything that he commanded him all the days of his life, except in the matter of Uriah the Hittite." According to an account in *The New York Times* of December 15, 1995, outraged Orthodox rabbis screamed at the foreign minister to "shut up." Another shouted, "You will not give out grades to King David!" A third man flew into such a rage of apoplexy that he had to be treated

for hypertension in the parliamentary infirmary, and a motion was introduced condemning the government for having besmirched the "sweet psalmist of Israel."[2]

As the story relates, any kind of criticism of David in Israel could cause a riot. Yet this sentiment denies the historical reality—at least as contained in the Bible—that David did in fact have Uriah killed to cover up his sexual indiscretion. Moreover, this approach undermines one of the basic themes in the Hebrew Bible: The children of Israel are the children of Israel precisely *because* they wrestle with God. The name given to Jacob, Israel, was given to him because he wrestled with God for his blessing. (The name Israel ["he contended with God"] is conferred on Jacob by a divine messenger after their struggle at the Wadi Jabbok [Gen. 32:28; Gen. 35:10; Hos. 12:3]. The twelve sons of Jacob and their tribal descendants are therefore called "the sons of Israel.") When we deny the reality of people's failings, we deny one of the truths the Bible wants us to confront when attempting to understand what it means to be a human being.

Skeletons can come in many shapes and sizes. For example, in a society like ours, where concern is great to strengthen families and uphold family values, it should appear on the surface scandalous that men like Peter left their families for the sole purpose of following Jesus. There is never any resolution raised in the Gospels about what would happen to the disciples' families when the men deserted them. If a man—or a woman for that matter—were to leave the family in order to follow an itinerant preacher in our day, we would not deem that person to be holy. We might believe that he or she was duped into joining a cult. We might believe that the person was an unfit spouse (and parent). We would not see this action as a noble deed. Nor was such an act seen as a noble deed in Jesus' day, either. In fact, the dubious morality of it all suggests that this behavior was a skeleton in the disciples' closets. We do not know if all the disciples were married, but we do know that Peter was. The other disciples did walk off their jobs, and they did leave their families. We should not overlook these issues when reading the texts.

Unfortunately (or maybe actually fortunately for us), no one in the Bible is beyond some sort of moral questioning. Remember, where there are people, there will be skeletons.

RULE OF THUMB 14: If the story sounds simple, then you can bet that the meaning isn't.

This rule of thumb applies mainly to the parables. We like to read the parables of Jesus because we believe that they are simple stories with simple, easily identifiable meanings. The only problem is that the Gospels themselves reject this idea.

For a good example of this disjunction between what we think the parables mean and what they *really* mean, let's look at Mark 4:13. After Jesus tells the well-known parable of the sower, his disciples and others come to him in private and ask him about its meaning. Apparently, they did not understand it when he initially told it. Their questions begin a discussion about who can and who cannot decipher the meaning of the parables. Only the insiders (the disciples) are to be given the secrets of the kingdom, which includes understanding the parables. The funny thing is, though, that Jesus' disciples still do not understand the parable. Their inability to "get it" prompts Jesus to say, "Do you not understand the parable? Then how will you understand all the parables?" (Mark 4:13). What does this mean? It means that the Gospels display a tension between what the disciples, the insiders, should understand as disciples and what outsiders will understand because they are outsiders. But the insiders *still* fail to understand the words of the Master, which is further highlighted in Mark 4:33, which reads, "With many such parables he spoke the word to them, as they were able to hear it; he did not speak to them except in parables, but he explained everything in private to his disciples." So, the study of parables has always intrigued scholars, because we are still not sure that the disciples—or even the early Christians for that matter!—understood the true meaning of the parables. Nor are scholars convinced that there is one true meaning that can be attached to a parable.

That multiple meanings can be derived from one parable can be illustrated by focusing new light on a well-known story, the parable of the Good Samaritan. It sounds simple enough.

> A man was going down from Jerusalem to Jericho, and fell into the hands of robbers, who stripped him, beat him, and went away, leaving him half dead. Now by chance a priest was going down that road; and when he saw him, he passed by on the other side. So likewise a Levite, when he came to the place and saw him, passed by on the other side. But a Samaritan while traveling came near him; and when he saw him, he was moved with pity. He went to him and bandaged his wounds, having poured oil and wine on them. Then he put him on his own animal, brought him to an inn, and took care of him. The next day he took out two denarii, gave them to the innkeeper, and said, "Take care of him; and when I come back, I will repay you whatever more you spend." (Luke 10:30–35)

The difficulty arises when we attempt to answer the question, What does the parable mean? The first thing to do is look at the context. The parable is set within the context of a debate about what the term "neighbor" means. Thus it is bracketed between two questions. The first comes from an anonymous lawyer, who asks, "And who is my neighbor?" (Luke 10:29). The second comes from Jesus, who asks, "Which of these three, do you think, was a neighbor to the man who fell into the hands of robbers?" (Luke 10:36). After the lawyer's response, Jesus tells him,

"Go and do likewise" (Luke 10:37). So, we then think that the meaning of the parable is: Do as the Samaritan did.

Some scholars, however, have raised the question of whether the parable always existed in the context in which we find it. What if Luke 10:30–35 was an independent story that was later put into its present context by Luke? What would the parable mean if that were the case? Well, the meaning of the parable could be different from "do as the Samaritan did." In order to determine this, scholars separate the parable from its context in the Gospel.

In order to understand the parable, one must understand the role and functions of the actors in the story. On the one hand, we have a Samaritan—the hero of the story—who has pity on the dying man. He approaches the man, helps him, and gives money on his behalf. On the other hand, we have the robbers—the villains of the story—who (along with the priest and the Levite) have no pity on the man. They take from the man, wound him, and leave him half dead. In other words, we have at least two sets of people taking opposite actions. The robbers do something socially reprehensible; they steal from the man. The Samaritan does something socially exemplary; he gives his own money on behalf of this person he does not know.

The priest and the Levite—the ones who turned down the possibility of being the hero in the story—are like the robbers in that they abandon the wounded man in his time of need. They do not steal from him as the robbers did, but they refuse to be inconvenienced or ritually defiled through contact with him. This is highlighted by the description in the story. The man is lying on the side of the road, in a ditch, in contrast to his original position, on the road. In fact, we are told in the story that the man who is robbed, the priest, and the Levite are all traveling on the same road from Jerusalem to Jericho. The man was "going down from Jerusalem to Jericho." The priest "was going down that road." Moreover, "[so] likewise a Levite, when he came to the place. . . . " This implies that the Levite was traveling on the same road as the man and the priest. By contrast, the Samaritan is described simply as "journeying," which does not suggest any particular direction. The same is true of the robbers: we do not know from which direction they have come or where they are going.

The cultural significance of the particular actors adds more meaning. Jewish people of religious conviction would have rejected both the robbers and the Samaritan. The robbers are those who break the commandment against stealing. Moreover, they represent those forces in society that attempt to tear apart the social order. Religious Jews considered a Samaritan a heretic, for he, too, represents the forces in society that were attempting to tear apart the religious aspects of the social order. He is like the modern-day cult member, who uses the Bible but understands it in a way that is considered unacceptable by the dominant religious forces.

In contrast, the priest and the Levite are clearly religious figures. They are the "right" kind of people, the kind of people we strive to be. As religious figures they represent stability in the social order. Furthermore, the fact that the man, the priest, and the Levite are on the road from Jerusalem to Jericho may be a way of telling us that orderly people follow orderly patterns of life—as opposed to the Samaritan and the robbers. In fact, the road may also indicate that the man who was robbed was a religious Jew. Jerusalem is not only the point of departure for the man, the priest, and the Levite, but also a symbol of "religion"—more specifically, the Jewish religion.

Given our expectations of religious people, we would expect either the priest or the Levite to help the wounded (possibly Jewish) man. Yet this is not the case. The Samaritan acts as the truly religious person would, even though he carries some of the same social and cultural baggage as the robbers. The priest and the Levite, on the other hand, act in some ways as the robbers do. They dare not venture out of their religiously ordered world (represented by the road). They claim the status of religious persons—and we identify them as such—but as long as they remain a priest and a Levite, they cannot help the wounded man in the ditch. Thus, the meaning of the parable is not "do as the Samaritan did"—because as religious people the priest and the Levite must be performing good deeds themselves—but "be as the Samaritan was."

Luke uses the parable as an example story (that is, a story that offers a pattern of correct behavior to emulate or wrong behavior to avoid), but apart from the context of the Gospel, the story means something more mysterious. Daniel Patte has suggested another explanation for the parable:

> The only possible answer in the context of the use of Scripture exemplified in the New Testament is that the parable was proposed as a paradigm for discovering the "signs of the kingdom." When one can discover, in the concrete situation in which he lives, a "good Samaritan," one is in the presence of a manifestation of the mysterious kingly activity of God. Yet this identification of the "good Samaritans" must be performed and verified with great care. There are many people performing good deeds who are not "Samaritans" (indeed, the "priests" and "Levites" certainly perform good deeds).[3]

The parable, then, is about how to identify a member of the kingdom. The good Samaritan was a member of the kingdom because he manifested the kingly activity of God. Clearly, the parable has a lot more meaning than just the one given to it by the writer of Luke.

The same can be said of many other parables in the Bible. They often have more meaning than we originally notice. The astute reader of the Bible will be careful not to come up with easy interpretations of parables that appear to be simple. The reader must dig deeper than the superficial meaning.

RULE OF THUMB 15: Everybody has an ax to grind.

Having an ax to grind is a familiar way of saying that each of us has our own perspective to promote. Biblical writers or editors were no different. They used the materials at their disposal to portray reality from their own perspectives. This rule of thumb is most helpful when we are reading the Hebrew Bible or the Gospels of the New Testament, but it can also be handy when we read other parts of the New Testament, as well. In modern biblical studies this rule of thumb is the basis for both redaction criticism and ideological criticism.

When reading the Bible we must be careful to pay special attention to the way the writers of the materials, as we now have them, selected, combined, and arranged already existing materials to express special concerns and emphasize certain issues. Redactors are interpreters of the materials out of which they structure a text and a theological perspective. The biblical writers drew upon certain ideas in the materials and rejected others. A good example of this is found in Galatians 3, where Paul drew upon materials related to the patriarch Abraham. In 3:6–9 he quoted Genesis and said, "Just as Abraham 'believed God, and it was reckoned to him as righteousness' [Gen. 15:6], so, you see, those who believe are the descendants of Abraham. And the scripture, foreseeing that God would justify the Gentiles by faith, declared the gospel beforehand to Abraham, saying, 'All the Gentiles shall be blessed in you' [Gen. 12:3]. For this reason, those who believe are blessed with Abraham who believed."

In highlighting the idea of Abraham as a man of faith, Paul was rejecting or discounting other aspects of the Abraham material that disagreed with the perspective he was trying to present. Some scholars believe that Paul was countering the view of Abraham presented by his own opponents.

Paul's opponents appear to have been teaching that true religious authority came from Abraham to the believers through the law. And judging from Paul's account of the conflict in Antioch (Gal. 2:11–14), the religious authority behind Paul's opponents was the Jerusalem church. This church, whose members included the apostles and Jesus' family members, was claiming to have more credible authority than the apostle Paul.

Paul's opponents apparently presented Abraham as an advocate of doing works of the law (see Gal. 3:2, 5). This understanding of Abraham came from scriptures like Genesis 18:19, where Abraham is shown instructing his children and household in the way of the Lord. In later Jewish literature, Abraham warns his offspring against forsaking practices like circumcision: "And great wrath from the Lord will be upon the sons of Israel because . . . they have not done the ordinance of this law because they have made themselves like the gentiles" (*Jub.* 15:34). In the Jewish wisdom book known as Sirach, the author maintains that Abraham kept the law (*Sir.* 44:20). To some religious persons, namely, Paul's opponents in Galatians, Abraham was best described as a pious, law-observant Jew.

Paul and his opponents agreed on some issues. For example, there does not seem to have been any disagreement between them about the inclusion of Gentiles in the promise of God. Likewise, they agreed that believers were children of Abraham in that they suffered trials and were expected to demonstrate faithfulness (cf. Gal. 4:29). Paul also encouraged the Galatians to identify with Abraham in rejecting idols (cf. 4:8–9). Furthermore, he encouraged them to show hospitality as Abraham did (cf. 4:14–15).

But it appears that Paul and his opponents parted company on the question of whether the Galatians should obey the law. Paul's understanding of Abraham was based on his perception that true religious authority (in this case, the promise) came directly from God. This was what the hearing

of faith in Galatians 3:2 and 3:5–6 means. From this understanding, Paul reconstructed the promise of Gentile inclusion—but with a twist. Instead of simply saying, *God* told
Abraham the Gentiles will be blessed in you, Paul recast
scripture and the gospel in this active role. In quoting Genesis 15:6, Paul was saying that faith overrode any concern for
participation in religious rituals like circumcision. This may
be why Paul never discussed Abraham's circumcision. He
did not want to cast any doubt on the importance of faith.
"[T]he law," Paul said, "does not rest on faith" (4:12).

Having established the importance of faith, Paul disposed of the idea that those who follow the law were the
offspring of Abraham by doing two things. First, he
excluded everyone except Christ from the possibility of
being the offspring of Abraham (3:16). He did this so that
he could argue that if there was any religious authority
that came from Abraham it was given to Christ, and so
could only be received from Christ. Second, Paul disposed
of the importance of the law in two ways: (1) he stressed
that the law came 430 years after the promise made to
Abraham (3:17), and (2) he emphasized that the law was
the very model of passed-on religious authority—being
"ordained through angels by a mediator" (3:19).

By speaking of Christ in this vague way (that is, as both
a historical person and as the corporate body of believers),
Paul was able to say both that Christ is the offspring of
Abraham and that the believers are part of the body of
Christ. He undercut his opponents' argument by beginning with a point on which they agreed but then used this
shared idea against them.

The ax that Paul had to grind in Galatians was over the
proper understanding of the Abraham tradition, and how
that tradition related to faith in Jesus. Paul intentionally
used material about Abraham that would champion his
"you do not need to be circumcised" perspective, while
ignoring or disregarding Abraham material that advocated

circumcision. By interpreting Abraham this way, Paul redacted the tradition so that circumcision became useless.

In the Hebrew Bible one way to understand the grinding of the ax is to look at the work of the Deuteronomistic editor. This editor assumed the perspective of the book of Deuteronomy, hence the name. In the Hebrew Bible we find a variety of theological perspectives (for example, the Yahwist, the Elohist, and the Priestly). The Deuteronomistic editor redacted these perspectives to bring them in line with his own. How? First, the Deuteronomistic editor saw the law and ethical living as more important than the stories that simply tell the history of Israel. Second, the Deuteronomistic perspective was based on the theology found in the book of Deuteronomy. Third, this redactor's work, called the Deuteronomistic history, introduced and expressed a history of Israel as it lived in the land of Canaan, and this history extended from Deuteronomy through Joshua, Judges, 1 and 2 Samuel, and 1 and 2 Kings.

The book of Deuteronomy challenges the people of God to be faithful to the principles of the ancestors, principles that had their origin in God. When the Northern Kingdom (Israel) was destroyed in 722 B.C.E., the Southern Kingdom (Judah) found itself unable to explain why God allowed Israel to be destroyed. An answer to Judah's question came in 622 B.C.E., when, reportedly, the book of Deuteronomy was found in the Jerusalem Temple. The theology of Deuteronomy was a major factor in a reform movement led by King Josiah and supported by a portion of the prophetic community of Jerusalem. King Josiah's reform was clearly based on the law code found in Deuteronomy 12–26. Unfortunately, this reform failed, and Judah fell to Babylon in 587 B.C.E. In exile, the Deuteronomistic editor, using the book of Deuteronomy as a theological guide, composed an interpretation of Israel's history in light of his understanding of Israel's and Judah's disobedience to God's covenant. His interpretation was that if the people had obeyed God's commands, they would have had prosperity and peace. But, because they disobeyed God's commands, they suffered hardship and defeat.

The editor, in writing his version of the history of Israel, used his sources in a particular way, that is, by interpreting them in light of the theology of Deuteronomy. Fortunately, he mentioned his sources for the reigns of the Israelite and Judean kings, citing, for example, sources such as "the book of the acts of Solomon" (1 Kings 11:41), "the Book of the Annals of the Kings of Israel" (1 Kings 14:19), and "the Book of the Annals of the Kings of Judah" (1 Kings 14:29). The editor combined these source materials with stories about prophets who often opposed the royal policies of the kings. Rather than merely chronicling the reigns of the kings, the Deuteronomistic editor interpreted them in light of his particular understanding of God's commitment to and claims on the people of Israel. In short, he created a new history—his own history—of the Israelites in Canaan.

Later, the writer of Chronicles wrote his own interpretation and application of the history, using many of the same materials that the Deuteronomistic editor had used, including the Deuteronomistic materials in Samuel and Kings. When you compare these two versions of Israelite history, you find that each understood the story in its own way. Generally speaking, the Deuteronomistic editor blamed the entire population for the downfall of the nation(s), while the chronicler blamed individual kings. The ax being ground in both cases concerns who is ultimately responsible for the downfall of the kingdoms.

Sometimes the ax being ground is more obvious than it is in the work the Deuteronomistic editor. For example, in the Gospel of Matthew we find an example of animosity between two groups—the developing Christian community and the Jewish community out of which it is developing:

[Jesus said,] "But woe to you, scribes and Pharisees, hypocrites! For you lock people out of the kingdom of heaven. For you do not go in yourselves, and when others are going in, you stop them. Woe to you, scribes and Pharisees, hypocrites! For you cross sea and land to make a single convert, and you make the new convert twice as much a child of hell as yourselves. Woe to you, blind guides, who say, 'Whoever swears by the sanctuary is bound by nothing, but whoever swears by the gold of the sanctuary is bound by the oath.' You blind fools! For which is greater, the gold or the sanctuary that has made the gold sacred?" (Matt. 23:13–17)

Are we to think that the scribes and Pharisees were actually as bad as they appear in this passage? Some scholars doubt it. Sources outside the Bible, like the Mishnah, give us a somewhat different picture of the scribes and Pharisees. Another way to understand this text is as an expression of a conflict between this new group of people, who will be called Christians, and the Jewish community, which did not accept the claim that Jesus was the messiah. It seemed like a foregone conclusion to some that Jesus was the messiah, but it was not readily apparent to everyone— even among some who knew Jesus! So this passage should be viewed not as an objectively accurate description of the scribes and Pharisees but as an account that is biased because of intercommunity conflict. Matthew is grinding the ax against the scribes and Pharisees in order to distinguish between "true" religion (developing Christianity) and "false" religion (Judaism as represented by this group). Often writers in the Bible do not present information in an unbiased manner but, rather, according to their convictions about what is right and true.

RULE OF THUMB 16: Cultures mix.

In the United States we are blessed with the opportunity to mix our many cultures. We mix hamburgers with tacos and flautas. We mix waltzes with merengue, salsa, the polka, and the lambada. We mix our understanding of "courage under fire" with *chutzpah*. We play bagpipes and bongo drums. In short, "American culture" is a blend of many cultural traditions, forms, and practices. Well, it was no different in the ancient world.

In biblical studies we call the mixing of cultures syncretism. Ancient Israelites, along with later Jews and Christians, were involved in this cultural mixing process. Such mixing can be detected throughout the Bible. A clear example can be found in the biblical languages. Parts of the Hebrew Bible are written in Aramaic, a Semitic dialect similar to Hebrew. The New Testament is written entirely in a dialect of Greek known as *koine*, which means "common." This fact itself says something about the early Christian movement, which began among Jews, who, we assume, did not speak, read, and write regularly in the Greek language. However, by the time the texts were written down, in order for one Christian to communicate with the majority of the Christian community, one had to write in Greek. Even Jews living outside of Judea needed a translation of the Bible that they could easily read and understand. This was the catalyst behind the writing of the Septuagint, a Greek translation of the Hebrew Bible.

To the astute reader, names in the Bible can indicate that cultural mixing has taken place. The book of Daniel, for instance, points out that the names of the three young men later cast into the fiery furnace, Shadrach, Meshach, and Abednego, were actually their Babylonian names and not their Hebrew names (Dan. 1:7). Esther—the hero of the Jewish people and the catalyst behind the festival of Purim—was so assimilated to the Persian way of life that it came as a shock to her husband, the king of Persia, to find out that she was in fact Jewish. Her Jewish name was Hadassah ("myrtle").

There are many other examples of how the Jews assimilated the culture and practices of their neighbors. One that most intrigues me is Isaiah 45:1, which reads, "Thus says the LORD to his anointed, to Cyrus. . . . " This is the only place in the Hebrew Bible in which God's anointed (i.e., messiah) is a non-Jew. Up to this point, God's messiah was always an Israelite—either the king (e.g., 1 Sam. 24:7) or the high priest (e.g., Lev. 4:3). This change appears to mean that despite the fact that the Jews were a conquered people and subject to the control of the Persians, there was little hostility between the two groups. As long as the Persians allowed the Jews to rebuild their temple and worship in peace, the Jews had no apparent problems with Persian government and culture. Some scholars believe that this situation was due to a prophecy spoken by Jeremiah: "Therefore thus says the LORD of hosts: Because you have not obeyed my words, I am going to send for all the tribes of the north, says the LORD, even for King Nebuchadrezzar of Babylon, my servant, and I will bring them against this land and its inhabitants, and against all these nations around; I will utterly destroy them, and make them an object of horror and hissing, and an everlasting disgrace" (Jer. 25:8–9). In any case, Jewish culture mixed with Babylonian and Persian culture, and these are just the easy examples to point out!

At times the mixing of cultures occurs in the background of a document. One of the things students find frustrating in studying the New Testament is the need to understand the Hellenistic world before you can actually start reading the biblical text. If, for example, you do not understand the Greco-Roman style of letter writing, then you will not understand Paul's letters. One of the keys to understanding Paul is understanding the ways in which his letters are like other letters of the period and the ways in which they are different. Knowing the nature of ancient letter writing can also assist one in determining what is and what is not a letter. Many scholars today believe, for example, that the book of Hebrews is not a letter but an exhortation or sermon of some sort. This insight can assist scholars in interpreting Hebrews, since the purpose of a sermon is somewhat different from that of a letter.

Sometimes ideas travel from one culture to another. Take, for example, Romans 6:7: "For whoever has died is freed from sin." Here Paul uses a Roman legal principle to explain the Christian idea of baptism. As a central Christian rite, baptism is understood by Paul to be an imitation of, or initiation into, Christ's death. He says, "Therefore we have been buried with him by baptism into death, so that, just as Christ was raised from the dead by the glory of the Father, so we too might walk in newness of life" (Rom. 6:4). This means that in baptism Christians symbolically die in order to be resurrected to a new life.

What Paul does not do is explain to the Roman Christians how this death means freedom from sin. This is where the Roman legal principle comes in. As a principle of law, a person cannot be punished for a crime after death. For example, a murderer who is convicted and executed for one crime cannot be tried and executed for another. A person can die only once, and so any outstanding crimes must be dismissed once a person dies. Nor can a person's friends and family be held responsible for his or her crime(s).

This is in direct contrast to other legal systems in which a person's family can be held responsible for outstanding crimes. We find this idea in the Hebrew Bible: "I the LORD your God am a jealous God, punishing children for the iniquity of parents, to the third and fourth generation of those who reject me" (Ex. 20:5). So Paul's perception of baptism and his use of this Roman principle are important for understanding Christian teaching on sin and redemption. Without the mixing of cultures at this point, it might have been impossible for Paul to communicate his teaching on baptism. Cultural mixing in the ancient world was not necessarily a bad thing, just as it is not considered a bad thing in our modern culture. It is simply a reality of life.

RULE OF THUMB 17: Always go for the more difficult reading.

This rule of thumb has to do with the practice of textual criticism. Note that by criticism, I mean "evaluation," the analysis of something with the intent of determining its value. Textual criticism is the process of evaluating biblical manuscripts for the purpose of determining the most likely original version of the text. The wording of manuscripts throughout the Jewish Scriptures and the Greek New Testament varies to a greater or lesser degree. Why do the manuscripts vary? They vary because they are all copies of the original, which is called the "autograph" in scholarly circles. Unfortunately, we do not possess the autographs of any of the texts. Thus, we must reconstruct the most likely original wording of the text, which scholars call the critical version of the text. This is part of the argument behind Rule of Thumb 4, "A translation is only as good as its translator."

Scholars use three classes of sources in the practice of textual criticism: (1) Greek and Hebrew manuscripts that have been preserved; (2) ancient translations of the Hebrew and Greek manuscripts into other languages (e.g., the Greek version of the Jewish Scriptures, called the Septuagint); (3) scriptural quotations made by rabbis and church fathers that appear in other writings we possess.

The *first step* in determining the "original" text is painstakingly to compare all the witnesses (or at least the important ones) in the three classes of texts noted above. From this, the scholar produces a compilation of the differing readings. This compilation is called a "critical apparatus." The process can shed light on how and why a scribe introduced a textual variation. The majority of variant readings occurred because of unintentional error. Accidental variations can result from one letter being mistaken for another; from the reversal of the sequence of two letters (*metathesis*); from substituting letters and words that sound similar; from confusing two successive lines that begin with the same letters or words (*homoeoarchton*) or that end with the same letters or words (*homoeoteleuton*), by allowing the eye to skip from the first to the second line (*parablepsis*), thus omitting the intermediate text (*haplography*); and from the eye accidentally processing the same word or groups of words twice so that the scribe writes for a second time a text that appeared only once in the original (*dittography*).

In some instances, the text may have been intentionally altered. Interestingly and ironically, scribes who thought about the text were more likely to make revisions than those who simply wanted to produce an accurate copy. Deliberate changes include correcting spelling and grammar; conforming a reading to a parallel passage; expanding or polishing a text by adding a familiar word or phrase where one seemed to be called for; combining similar phrases; clarifying historical and geographical problems; substituting synonymous words or expressions; and modifying or deleting expressions considered objectionable by the scribe.

The astute reader's fundamental considerations when assessing variant readings involve analyzing both external and internal evidence. External evidence relates to the date of the witnesses, the geographical distribution of the witnesses who agree, and the family relationship of manuscripts and groups of witnesses, if that can be determined. Internal evidence is concerned with (1) transcriptional (i.e., having to do with the printed matter) probabilities, which require analysis of the details of ancient writing styles and the scribe's habits, and (2) intrinsic (i.e., having to do with subjective considerations used to evaluate the reading "in its context," taken in the broadest sense of the word) probabilities, which necessitate examining the author's style and vocabulary throughout the book.

The fact that different conclusions are drawn by textual critics can usually be traced to their individual judgments as to what must be deemed most significant. For the Hebrew Bible, for example, most scholars use a manuscript called the Masoretic text as a point of departure for textual criticism, because it is a complete, established text that was scrupulously transcribed. In some cases, however, readings in the Qumran Hebrew manuscripts are considered superior to the Masoretic text by virtue of their agreement with ancient translations. The Qumran manuscripts, however, are not complete, and some were negligently copied. So it is important to remember that the text-critical method is not cut and dried.

As a general rule, the more difficult reading is usually to be preferred. (By this I mean, when reconstructing a manuscript, text critics prefer grammatically difficult readings to easier ones, and also prefer the less smooth or unassimilated reading—since in both instances scribes resisted the urge to produce a more polished, harmonious text. The shorter reading is also favored by the majority of textual scholars (unless specific omissions can be traced to *homoeoteleuton*, or unless the shorter reading does not conform to the character, style, or scope of the author), because scribes tended to supplement the text with explanations or material from parallel passages rather than to abridge it. Simply stated, the reading that best explains the origin of the other readings should be preferred as the original.

For beginners in academic biblical study, such considerations are not a major part of the program of interpretation. However, as you advance in your attempt to understand the Bible, you will find that there are variations in biblical texts. These variations can have a significant effect on the reading. An example can be found in Romans 10:17. On the one hand, in the KJV the verse reads, "So then, faith [cometh] by hearing, and hearing by the word of God." If you were to look at the critical apparatus, you would find that the manuscripts that support this rendition of the text go back to, primarily, the fifth and sixth centuries, with the earliest rendition occurring in the fourth century.

On the other hand, in the NRSV the same verse reads, "So then faith comes from what is heard, and what is heard comes through the word of Christ." The critical apparatus on this rendition says that the majority of these manuscripts come primarily from the fourth century. Also, a number of ancient church fathers quote the verse as saying "word of Christ." The differences in interpreting the passage are important when "God" is substituted for "Christ" and vice versa. The "word of God" rendering of the passage could suggest that faith comes from hearing (or reading) the Bible, the word of God, while the "word of Christ" rendering strongly suggests that persons come to faith by means of hearing the preached gospel. Scholars have decided that the more original rendering of the passage is "word of Christ," according to the principles I outlined above, particularly the principle that calls for the preference of the more difficult reading. Again, the assumption of scholarship is that the more difficult reading is the more original, because scribes and editors tended to try to make reading the text easier instead of more difficult.

RULE OF THUMB 18: The "accidents of history" don't necessarily prove anything.

History is not a predetermined course of events that have meaning apart from the interpretation we give them. In this regard, the "accidents of history" are those events that we may take to be meaningful but whose meaning is not predetermined. For example, if I am driving my car and have an accident, I could take that to mean that my driving skills are not good. Or I could take it to mean that God was somehow punishing me for some error or sin I committed. Or I could take it to mean that the driving skills of the other individual are not good. The so-called real meaning of the event is in doubt because the event does not lend itself to a clear interpretation. Any of the possible interpretations could be true.

The guiding force of biblical study cannot be possibility, however, because possibilities abound. Rather, the guiding force must be probability. That is, given the event described, it is the task of the astute reader to determine what the most probable meaning of the event is.

As I noted in Rules 9 and 15, biblical writers were not in the business of offering unbiased interpretations of events. Their concern was to transmit faith and convictions along with facts. This creates a huge problem for those of us who are attempting to understand what an event signifies outside of the interpretation given it by the writers, if such an understanding is possible at all. This problem is only confounded when the occurrence of the event itself is in question. Let us take two examples to illustrate this point.

In Exodus 12:37 we read that 600,000 Hebrew men, along with women, children, and a "mixed group" of people, left Egypt in the exodus. This means that a population of more than a million people, the equivalent of the entire population of Indianapolis or Nashville, decided to leave Egypt at one time. This estimate is highly improbable for a number of reasons. First, migrations of that size are almost impossible to orchestrate. Remember, we are talking about an era without megaphones or other modern tools that would assist in such a movement. Second, a migration of that enormity would have been recorded by someone. Yet there is no record of such a movement of population outside of the Bible. Third, a group that large would have left all sorts of garbage along the way. Yet there is no archaeological trace of such a group. Consequently, although scholars believe that some sort of migration from Egypt took place, they seriously doubt that the number was so high.

The implication of this for our rule of thumb is clear. In this case, the accident of history is the migration of the Hebrews from Egypt to Israel. Few scholars question the veracity of such a migration. However, the migration event itself does not prove the authenticity of the number of Hebrews who left.

Is it possible that approximately one million people got up one day and left Egypt en masse? Yes.

Is it *probable* that so many people would have accomplished such a feat almost four thousand years ago? No.

Does that mean that the exodus did not take place? No.

Another example comes from the ministry of Jesus. In Mark we meet a Jesus who is a healer and exorcist. People flock to him to be healed and to have demons cast out of themselves and their friends. They see Jesus, we are led to believe, in a positive light. But other people in the community think that Jesus is not a good person. They say, "He has Beelzebul, and by the ruler of demons he casts out demons" (Mark 3:22). In short, it is not clear what the interpretation of Jesus' healing activities should be. Some believed that Jesus was a healer and exorcist, while others believed that he was a charlatan. The events were the same, but the interpretations were different. This tension helps us understand that events do not make their own meanings, but, rather, that meanings are a result of the interpretations given them by human beings.

The biblical scholar Gotthold Lessing offered the best explanation of this fact regarding the accidents of history. Lessing argued correctly that revelation may come through history (e.g., the revelation of the gospel through Jesus Christ), but truth cannot be established by proofs from historical facts. He called this chasm between history and faith an "ugly ditch." Some would say that such a gap between faith and history is merely a function of the passage of time. However, Lessing said it is much more than that. The problem, he argued, is not just the passage of time, but the absence of the spirit and power that must have accompanied the original event: "The problem is that this proof of the spirit and of power [i.e., the event] no longer has any spirit or power, but has sunk to the level of *human testimonies of spirit and power*."[4]

Lessing argued that even if he could be certain about the historical events attributed to persons like Jesus, that certainty could not prove the ground for faith. He asked, "If on historical grounds I have no objection to the statement that this Christ himself rose from the dead, must I therefore accept it as true that this risen Christ was the Son of God?"[5] His answer was No. From this, Lessing concluded that "accidental truths of history can never become the proof of necessary truths of reason."[6] In other words, historical events or reminiscences of historical events do not *necessarily* prove the authenticity of the *meanings* we attach to those events. Rule of Thumb 18 is difficult to accept, but it is fundamental to the academic study of the Bible.

RULE OF THUMB 19: Don't argue what you can't prove.

Neither you nor I can prove *conclusively* that Jericho fell after Joshua and his troops walked around its perimeter for seven days, so I caution my students not to base the truthfulness of their arguments or their faith on Jericho's ruin. Likewise, other aspects of the Hebrew Bible seem improbable when you reflect on them carefully. For example, the traditional ascription of the first five books of the Bible to Moses is improbable. It is improbable because the book of Deuteronomy tells of Moses' death, and how could a person write about his own death? Moreover, the title of the book itself is suspicious. Deuteronomy is a

Greek term that means "second law" or "second retelling of the law." Why would the law need to be retold when the Israelites had not had the opportunity to live out or live by the first telling of the law?

The book of Genesis tells of the creation of the world and the primeval history of humanity. Moses was not there. He would not be born for more than a thousand years. So how could we reasonably lay emphasis upon his telling of the story when the Bible itself tells us that Moses was educated by the Egyptians? He did not even find out that he was a Hebrew until he was grown, and nowhere does it say that Moses was instructed in the Hebrew version of the history of the world. We cannot take things for granted. We must place them under scrutiny and argue only for what we can reasonably prove.

This rule of thumb takes us back to our *possibility* versus *probability* argument (see Rule of Thumb 18). There is an irony in the fact that the same students who argue that faith is not based on empirical evidence often insist on the historical authenticity of the events described in the Bible. Some scholars argue similarly. Without objective proof, these scholars argue, you cannot tell theological truth from theological error. When they speak of evidence or "the testability of religious assertions," they mean something more than what scholars call "permissive evidence." They mean evidence that incontrovertibly proves the existence and activity of God. I shall not attempt anything that grand. Rather, I want to address the construction of arguments themselves.

The Construction of Arguments

Whenever we claim that something is true or correct, we are making an argument. By its very nature, argument is open to question and debate.

> Whenever a man makes a claim to knowledge he lays himself open to the challenge that he should make his claim good, justify it. In this respect, a claim to knowledge functions simply as an assertion carrying special emphasis and expressed with special authority. To meet this challenge, he must produce whatever grounds or argument he considers sufficient to establish the justice of his claim. When this is done, we can settle down and criticise his argument, using whichever categories of applied logic are called for in the nature of the situation.[7]

In other words, when you make a statement you should be able to explain the reasoning behind the statement that you believe makes it valid. This is what reasoning is all about. If we want to hold on to our beliefs in a critically defensible way, we must provide ourselves with "reasons" for their acceptance. When a roommate challenges one of your beliefs, you may find that you have no very solid reasons to offer in its support. Before now, you may never have had to go beyond the premise that "well, everybody believes it." Since your roommate will not find that statement true or sufficient, you are left with three choices: (1) develop valid reasons for your position; (2) abandon your position quickly; or (3) fall back on some inflexibly dogmatic position. The choice is yours, but I believe that most people want to be able reasonably to defend their most cherished beliefs. In fact, a "reasoned" judgment is a judgment in defense of which you can produce adequate and appropriate reasons.

Almost all arguments have three phases. They can be outlined as follows: (1) the statement of a *claim*, (2) the support of the claim with *evidence* or testimony, and (3) a *verdict* or judgment pronounced on the claim. Each of these phases (claim, evidence, and verdict) is important to the persuasiveness of the overall argument. This being the case, you must be careful not to claim more than the evidence will reasonably allow. In order to determine this, we need to discuss the elements of an argument itself.

Claims

A claim is an assertion that is put forward publicly for general acceptance. Putting forth a claim implies that underlying "reasons" can demonstrate the claim to be "well founded" and thus entitled to be generally accepted. The claim is the "destination" of the argument. So the first thing we need to do when constructing, analyzing, and criticizing an argument is to understand the precise character of that destination. This means asking questions like: What exactly are we discussing? After hearing the argument, where am I supposed to stand on this issue? At what time or position must I consider agreeing as to the outcome of the argument?

Grounds

Once you have determined what the claim is, you must consider what kind of underlying foundation is required for the claim to be accepted as sound and reliable. Grounds are statements that specify particular facts about a situation. These facts are already accepted as true and can thus be relied upon to clarify and make good the previous claim. This means we must ask ourselves questions like: What information is the author going on? On what grounds is the claim based? Where must we ourselves begin if we are to see whether we can take the step the author proposes and so end by agreeing to the author's claim? In any argument, the person making the claim must begin by producing at least minimal grounds for the claim in the form of some first set of undisputed facts that is neither "too little" nor "too shaky" to persuade the reader or hearer. Unless we can satisfy this fundamental requirement, we will not be able to fulfill what the legal system calls our *burden of proof*. The kind of evidence necessary to prove a claim will vary from case to case, but one thing will remain constant: The claim under discussion can be no stronger than the grounds that provide its foundation.

Warrants

Knowing the grounds for your claim is only the first step in constructing or analyzing the solidity of an argument. Next we must determine that these grounds provide genuine support for this particular claim and are not just irrelevant information. This is where warrants come in. Warrants are statements that indicate how the facts (grounds) on which we agree are connected to the claim we are offering. The next set of questions to ask is: Given where the argument started, how do you justify the move from these grounds to that claim? What road do you take to get from this starting point to that destination? The warrant of our argument is what entitles us to be confident that, in this particular case, the step from grounds to claim is a generally reliable one. Warrants can be called by different names in different disciplines. I call them "rules of thumb," but they may also be principles, laws of nature, values, customs, or procedures.

Think of an argument as a cake. The grounds are the ingredients of the cake, and the warrant is the general recipe used to combine those ingredients into the finished product, the claim.

Backing

Warrants themselves cannot be taken totally on trust. Once we know what rule of thumb, formula, or principle is being relied on in any argument, the next set of questions must be raised: Is this really a safe move to make? Does this route take us to the required destination securely and reliably? What other general information do you have to back up your trust in this particular warrant? This is what is called backing. Backing means the generalizations that make explicit the body of experience that is relied on to establish the trustworthiness of the arguments applied in a particular case. In general, the backing for a warrant will always be longer and more complex than a simple description of grounds or a statement of the rule on which the present argument relies.

Using this discussion of arguments, let's go back to our example of the fall of Jericho. The claim in this case is that the walls of Jericho collapsed after Joshua and the Israelites marched around them for seven days. The grounds for this claim are the story told in Joshua 6:1–27 and archaeological evidence that indicates that Jericho at some time in its history was conquered in a manner similar to that described in the Bible. The warrant most often appealed to in this argument is that the Hebrew Bible seeks to relate objectively the history of the Israelites. The backing for this warrant is that the Bible is the word of God, and that as the word of God it would not seek to mislead or deceive the reader. The Bible is a trustworthy witness to the words and deeds of God, who, because of God's unbiased and trustworthy nature, can be relied upon to communicate the revelation found in scripture in a historically accurate fashion. So, in the end, the truth of the destruction of Jericho rests on the character of God and not *necessarily* on the verifiability of the event. This is the general construction of the argument.

Ultimately basing an interpretive argument on a theological claim (i.e., that the character of God affirms the trustworthiness of scripture) is certainly one of the ways to attempt to understand scripture. However, it is not the general starting point of biblical scholarship. As I said in chapter 1, in its method, biblical scholarship begins by suspending the existing interpretation of the text in order to determine if the text really says what the doctrine claims. (This goes back to Rule of Thumb 1.) So biblical scholars begin an analysis of a text (or an event described by a text) in the same way a historian or literary critic or other scholar would. In this case, the first thing the scholar notes is that the evidence for the destruction of Jericho by Joshua and his forces is sketchy. This is not, necessarily, a problem, though. It is often reasonable to base your conclusions on something less than *absolutely* perfect evidence. What we will examine here are the formal connections in the argument to see if they stand up to investigation.

Let us begin with the grounds for the claim, because here is where we bear the burden of proof. First, the primary evidence for the destruction of Jericho by the Israelites comes from Joshua 6. Evidence internal to the book indicates that it was written at a time long after the event supposedly took place. Most scholars agree that the book of Joshua owes its formation to the Deuteronomistic editor. That is, the Deuteronomist has determined the overall presentation of the book. Individual stories may have circulated prior to the time the book was put together, but the presentation *as we now have it* is a creation of the author. Scholars also note that the stories in the first part of the book, Joshua 2–11, are etiological in character (that is, they are stories that attempt to explain the causes or origins of a modern situation) and try to make more of a theological point than a historical one.

The history of the book of Joshua is further complicated by the fact that some traditions in Judges 1 present a completely different picture of events. And the archaeological evidence does not settle the matter. Jericho was destroyed. A cataclysmic destruction did take place, but the evidence also demonstrates that Jericho's destruction occurred long before the Israelite invasion, if the traditional dating of the exodus is considered to be correct. So the evidence (grounds) for the claim regarding Jericho's destruction is shaky at best. Given this, it appears irrational to argue that the dubious character of the grounds for our claim should be overlooked, based on our warrant that the Hebrew Bible seeks to relate the history of Israel in an objective manner. (See Rule of Thumb 15 on the question of the Bible's objectivity.)

In the end, the best way to understand what the story of Jericho's destruction is trying to tell us may be to read it in light of Rule of Thumb 10: The importance of the story may lie in the activity of God and God's people, rather than in the historical verifiability of the event.

When constructing arguments based on the Bible, we must be careful not to argue for things we cannot reasonably prove. Constructing an argument about a biblical passage involves much more than the Bible itself. The biblical evidence is just one of the components that must be considered in a good argument. Furthermore, as Rule of Thumb 18 tells us, proving the historicity of an event does not make the meaning of that event self-evident.

3

Rules of Thumb for Understanding Biblical Scholarship

RULE OF THUMB 20: Most biblical scholars can't agree on lunch, much less the precise meaning of a text.

This rule of thumb sounds negative in its assessment, but that is not my intent. My goal is, in fact, the opposite. I am attempting to lay to rest your fears regarding conflicting scholarly opinions. Scholars do not, and will not, agree for a number of reasons. Sometimes they disagree about the usefulness of certain methods of biblical research. At other times they disagree over the interpretation of the evidence, for example, what warrants (see Rule of Thumb 19) inform the movement from grounds to claim. One of the main reasons scholars disagree is religious commitment. Like many other people who study the Bible, biblical scholars are often motivated by their religious commitments, and those commitments may guide their reading of the biblical texts. To the Reformer, Martin Luther, the doctrine of justification by faith through grace was the most important doctrine in all of scripture, and especially in the writings of Paul. So a Lutheran scholar might read Paul's letters to the Romans and Galatians and emphasize Paul's argument for justification by faith through grace. In fact, many of the world's leading Pauline scholars, until recently, were of German extraction. This makes sense, given Paul's importance in Lutheranism.

What I will do now is highlight three areas in which scholarly opinion differs because of three "prejudices" brought by scholars to the text: (1) the idea that the Bible has something important to say to people of faith, (2) reactions to other scholars' religious commitments, and (3) the belief held by some scholars that religion itself is illegitimate.

1. What underlies scholars' personal interests in certain aspects, ideas, or persons in scripture is a fundamental reality of biblical study: *People read the Bible because they believe it has something important to say to them*. You are thinking, of course, that, yes, the Bible has something important to say to us: It is the word of God. But I am trying to highlight a general idea that is deeper than that: Unless it has been given as a class assignment, we each, as human beings, come to any piece of literature, biblical or not, with the presupposition that what is going to be said in this text is going to be important to *me* somehow. In other words, we read the Bible precisely because it has been identified as the word of God, and so we believe that God tells us something important in it. We come to the text with certain ideas, questions, or concerns that we want answered.

To take this one step further, because of our religious backgrounds, we often have an idea of what the Bible will say about our concerns—or at least we think we do. These can be called "prejudices," because we have in some sense pre-judged what the Bible is going to say. Prejudices are *not* bad things. In fact, they are what motivate us to engage the text in the first place! We must be willing, however, to confront and determine the reality of our prejudices in order to test them accurately against the witness of scripture itself. This is true for student as well as scholar.

Our prejudices largely determine what we look for in scripture. For example, I enjoy studying early Christian reflections on worship practices. Part of my concern in studying Christian prayer, for instance, has to do with what I believe are questions fundamental to religious phenomena in general: Why do people want to worship in this way? What do they expect to accomplish through this activity? Why do they think God seeks to be worshiped in this way? I am also interested in understanding how certain ideas develop around worship practices, and how those ideas are transmitted and modified through the tradition. Therefore, in my approach to and reading of certain biblical texts I bring that array of questions, and I seek to answer them. These questions help determine the kind of analysis I bring to bear on the text and, thus, the type of interpretation I develop from it.

These prejudices on my part probably derive from by Methodist upbringing. Methodists place great importance on the practice of piety. Since antiquity, piety has been coupled with the performance of certain rituals. So, although some non-Methodists might view the Methodist concern for piety as a type of "works righteousness" (that is, a belief that good works help us merit salvation, as opposed to a belief that salvation rests solely on a person's faith), Methodist tradition sees piety as part of the overall process of sanctification (that is, becoming holy), by means of which we become the persons God calls us to be. In short, like scientists developing and testing a hypothesis, biblical scholars come to the text with an idea they seek to prove or disprove.

Motivations like this from outside the text play as large a part in interpretation as does the text itself. Unfortunately, scholars do not often communicate such underlying personal concerns explicitly in their analysis of the text, and students frequently have difficulty recognizing what the interpreter brought to the text. More tragic than this, too many scholars operate under the illusion that their scholarship is completely objective. Thus, Rule of Thumb 15 ("Everybody has an ax to grind") applies to reading biblical scholarship as well as reading the Bible itself.

2. On the other side of the theological coin, biblical scholarship can also be motivated by a reaction against certain kinds of religious commitments. A good example of such scholarship is the book *Paul among Jews and Gentiles*, by Lutheran bishop and scholar Krister Stendahl. This book was as much a reaction to his religious upbringing as it was a study in concepts central to the theology of the apostle Paul. Stendahl's central conviction in the book is that readings of Paul—particularly Protestant ones— have emphasized certain doctrines (e.g., justification by faith) out of proportion to their actual prominence in Paul's thought. Furthermore, he argues, many interpreters overlook Paul's actual language in order to homogenize him into the wider Christian tradition. Stendahl wants to make the point that Paul was different from his Christian contemporaries. Stendahl's desire to highlight the differences between Paul's thought and (later) homogenized Christian thought served as the rationale behind some of his chapter headings: "Call Rather Than Conversion," "Justification Rather Than Forgiveness," and "Love Rather Than Integrity."

The book is interesting in part because it exposes the ways by which scholars have read Paul through later doctrinal lenses rather than attempting to understand Paul (as best we can) on his own terms. In one interesting passage, Stendahl addresses the sometimes unconscious prejudices that guide the readings of both students and scholars of the Bible:

Many of us read the Bible all on one level. One reason for this may be that we are somewhat afraid that unless we do this the word of God is not going to be relevant for us. We do not have enough faith in the word of God really to allow it to speak for itself—so we hang on our own little relevancies, just as apples and other decorations are hung on a Christmas tree. Actually, there is no greater threat to serious biblical studies than a forced demand for "relevance." We must have patience and faith enough to listen to and seek out the original's meaning. If this is not done, biblical study suffers and may, indeed, come up with false and faulty conclusions and interpretations.[8]

The value of disagreement in biblical scholarship rests on the insight that what scholars bring to the study of the Bible is much more than just a disciplined way to approach the material. Varying interpretations give us the opportunity to judge the relevance of a scholar's claims regarding the text under investigation. To put it another way, since all interpretation is more or less based on one's perspective, the addition of a contrary perspective to one's own may help us see that our present interpretation is not the only one that can be gleaned from the text. Confronting an opposing perspective should encourage us either to (a) strengthen our thesis in light of this new argument or (b) abandon our thesis because it does not accurately represent the evidence.

3. At times, scholars have more at stake in their interpretations than just correcting faulty explanations. Somewhat surprisingly, some scholars have as their ultimate goal exposing the illegitimacy of religion itself. They are convinced that the claims of religion are actually the function of phenomena that are nonreligious in nature. They argue that the "something out there" that religion posits is not really real, does not really exist. And so they use the tools of the discipline to demonstrate the reality of their conviction. Oftentimes this upsets students, because they do not easily realize that a good critic can be your best friend.

Critics point out the inconsistencies and weaknesses in our arguments. When critics deny that what religious people claim to be real is truly real, this is good for the ongoing vitality of religious belief, because the critics force us to confront issues that we may avoid otherwise. Moreover, areligious biblical scholars confirm the validity of biblical studies as an academic enterprise. To borrow a phrase from Schubert Ogden, a well-known theologian, this phenomenon represents "the strange witness of unbelief":[9] the failure on the part of areligious persons to establish any clear distinction between their real confidence in the ultimate meaning of human life and the faith in God they claim to deny.

A New Testament scholar need not be Christian in order for that scholar's conclusions to be valid. For years Christians have studied the Hebrew Bible (or Old Testament), the Qur'an, and other sacred writings of the world's religions, often without an eyebrow being raised as to the validity of their interpretations. Likewise, an American scholar of French history can be just as competent as a French one. In such a situation the idea of scholarship as embracing a certain *discipline* becomes extremely important, for if the methods of investigation in the discipline are followed, the scholarship is valid. An areligious biblical scholar may "see" aspects of the text that the religious biblical scholar may not see. A religious biblical scholar who can acknowledge the validity of another's interpretations has the advantage of being able to interpret the text in a manner that strives for the greatest degree of objectivity.

Is it prudent to reject an interpretation of a text because it may conflict with one's current beliefs, understandings, or practices? No. In fact, that may be even more reason to engage it. The contrary opinions of academics are not indicative of the failure of biblical scholarship. Rather, they demonstrate the vitality of biblical scholarship. So, when academics disagree as to the meaning of a biblical text, do not throw up your hands in disgust, despair, or frustration. Take it as an opportunity to enter into the debate yourself. Seize the initiative and use your ability for thoughtful analysis (firmly adhering to Rules of Thumb 18 and 19) as a way of understanding what the Bible is trying to communicate.

RULE OF THUMB 21: Where you start often determines where you end.

This rule of thumb is actually a concise way of saying that (1) all methods of interpretation have their limitations, and (2) extratextual matters often determine the scope and character of the investigation. Let me explain.

First, all methods of biblical interpretation are limited because of the kinds of questions they generate. For example, the historical method is oriented toward questions involving historical context: Who? What? When? Where? Why? The goals of the method are explanation and understanding. This means that the historical critic seeks to understand a given biblical text in light of the historical context in which it was written. History, the past, what the text meant at the time it was written, become the agenda. Other questions or concerns are, by necessity, left out because they cannot be addressed by this method.

Historical criticism has become more sophisticated, but its limitations persist. A good example of its limitations can be found in a paper I wrote on petitionary prayer in antiquity and the relationship of that form of prayer to the petition for bread in the Lord's Prayer.[10] I began by analyzing the philosophical and theological issues surrounding petitionary prayer in Greco-Roman and Jewish religion, and the way those non-Christian reflections on prayer informed the early Christian understanding of prayer. I then looked at the petition for bread in the Lord's Prayer. By looking at bread as a symbol of divine and human cooperative productivity, I explained how the symbol of bread fit into the religious context of its time. I also demonstrated how the petition for bread in the Lord's Prayer was part of the larger Christian discussion on material goods. In essence, I explained what the petition meant at the time of its composition.

I did not (and could not), however, address the way in which petitionary prayer should be understood today. That is, I did not ask such questions as, What kinds of material goods are appropriate for the modern Christian to request? Does the symbol of bread carry the same meaning today as it did in ancient times? Given the type of analysis I was conducting, these questions would not have been entirely appropriate. The ancient world was very different from ours, and some of our modern concerns were not their concerns.

This does not mean, however, that by learning about the past we have not learned something about the present. We most certainly have. Yet ancient understandings are not easily appropriated into the modern world. So, while historical analysis is beneficial because it gives us a fuller understanding of the past, another type of analysis is necessary to determine if what was true then can be considered true and worthy of imitation in the present.

Second, prejudices and presuppositions play as important a role in textual investigation as does the method employed. (This point is connected in many ways with Rule of Thumb 20.) Furthermore, the context in which the investigation is conducted may also play an important role in the scope and character of the analysis. As I said earlier, the prejudices of scholars and students often determine what they look for in a biblical text, that is, how they approach that text. In a manner similar to scientific investigation, the student of the Bible forms an idea in his or her mind regarding what the author is trying to say. Sometimes this idea is nothing more specific than a "hunch" or vague insight that must subsequently be proved or disproved. If this hypothesis were to become the sole guiding principle behind the investigation, the analysis might become too narrow in scope. This danger is part of the reason scholarship relies on dialogue and conversation among researchers in the field.

Let me give you an example from my dissertation. In it, I argued that the reason Clement of Alexandria does not analyze the Lord's Prayer in his treatise on prayer is because he rejects it as the proper prayer for a Christian. In conversation, a colleague raised a question regarding that central hypothesis. My colleague said that the grounds for my dissertation were more than sound, that I demonstrated that Clement knew the Gospel of Matthew, the Sermon on the Mount, and the Lord's Prayer, and that Clement developed his treatise on prayer in contradistinction to the Lord's Prayer. Although the warrants that allowed me to move from grounds to claim appeared valid, my analysis involved an argument from silence. That is, Clement never explicitly says that he developed his idea of prayer over against the idea presented in the Lord's Prayer. Since silence is inscrutable, my hunch that Clement of Alexandria rejected the Lord's Prayer appeared valid.

On the other hand, countered my colleague, was it not also possible, since silence is inscrutable, that Clement simply rejected the Lord's Prayer for the "enlightened" Christian? Well, yes, that is another way to interpret the silence. We lack the evidence needed to determine the most accurate interpretation. If Clement had objected to the use of the Lord's Prayer in the worship life of the church, then we could be sure that he rejected the Lord's Prayer altogether. If Clement had said that the Lord's Prayer was said in his church and he said it along with his fellow worshipers, even though he did not believe it to be worthwhile, then we would know that he disapproved of its use by the "enlightened" Christian. Unfortunately, this helpful evidence does not exist, and so I must leave open the possibility that there is another way to understand Clement's not using the Lord's Prayer in his discussion on prayer. In other words, dialogue helps us clarify and broaden our intellectual models.

As I said in my discussion of Rule of Thumb 19, we are often forced to base our claims on less than perfect or con-clusive evidence. So discussion and testing claims is important. Because we can so easily fall into a mind-set that convinces us that we are right, we must be careful consistently to test our hypotheses against the thoughtful reflections of others. We often begin our investigation with an idea that we seek to prove, and proving this idea can sometimes cause us to lose sight of arguments that can be raised to the contrary.

As I said, the context in which a scholarly investigation is conducted can also play an important role in the way the investigation is carried out. For example, there is just as much need for accuracy in interpretation in a sermon as there is in an academic presentation. Both the scholar and the preacher are under certain obligations to tell the truth to their audiences, that is, to interpret accurately the text, using the best methods at their disposal. What may work in the classroom, however, may not work in the sanctuary. Preachers have the additional obligation to make the text they are interpreting relevant to people gathered in the church. This means that the preacher must place the text and its interpretation within the context of the modern human experience to which the congregants can relate. Otherwise, the text will lose its relevance.

The academic, on the other hand, is not *necessarily* under the obligation to make the text under consideration relevant to the modern human experience. Biblical scholars do place the text within the context of human experience, but often the context is the human experience of the past. Furthermore, understanding past human experience can mean detailed analysis of aspects of that experience that are foreign to us today. So the context in which the investigation takes place can determine its very scope and character.

To overcome the problems related to this rule of thumb, we must keep uppermost in our minds that our methods of analysis can address only certain questions we seek to have answered by the text. So when reading the work of a biblical scholar, we must keep in mind the method the scholar uses. Furthermore, we must keep in mind the fact that scholars do not approach a text blindly, as if it were assigned by a committee. No, scholars use certain texts because they believe that they understand what the text means, or they believe that the text supports a claim they are trying to prove. This means that when reading biblical scholarship we must engage the argument of the author. We should ask ourselves questions like, What kind of evidence is the author overlooking? Does the claim the author is advancing try to do too much? Does the author take contrary evidence into account? Is there another way of looking at this text that still remains true to the principles of biblical scholarship? (At times the answers to these questions can be found in the footnotes of the article or book, because that is where the "conversation" with other scholars occurs.) When this type of engagement with a scholar's work occurs, we put the scholar's argument on trial and judge it according to the prevailing standards of biblical research. In this manner we can avoid, as much as possible, the problem this rule of thumb envisions.

RULE OF THUMB 22: In the commentary game, older is not always better.

The best way to begin discussion of this rule of thumb is to define our main term, "commentary." A commentary is a sustained interpretation of a biblical text. Usually a commentary focuses on a complete book, such as the Gospel of Matthew or the book of Deuteronomy. Less often, a commentary deals with certain parts of what is now considered a complete text, such as a recent commentary on the author known as Second Isaiah, who heretofore has usually been discussed in commentary volumes on the complete book of Isaiah. A commentary can also deal with a particular body of literature, such as the Prophets. At any rate, what makes a commentary fit the definition is that the literature under consideration logically appears to belong together.

What is most useful about commentaries is that they attempt to demonstrate and make sense out of the relationship between a particular text within a book, such as a Gospel, and the entire book itself. We've all heard the saying "He cannot see the forest for the trees." Essentially, for the biblical scholar, a commentary must connect the trees (the elements of a text) and the forest (the entirety of the text). In other words, there must be a logical and coherent connection between the individual verses that make up a work and the work itself.

However, a commentary must help you to see the trees as well as the forest. This means that, in writing a commentary, a scholar is obligated to concentrate on and sufficiently explain the particular verses that make up a biblical book. I am suspicious of very short commentaries, because they usually lack the depth of analysis needed really to understand a verse of scripture, not to mention an entire biblical book. If interpreting the Bible is the goal of biblical scholarship, scholars must use all the acumen they have developed to communicate the meaning of a text (whether a verse or the entire work).

Commentaries are important guides to our overall understanding of the Bible. They often represent the fullness of scholarship at the time of their writing. Yet that fullness eventually may become a commentary's weakness, and it explains why we must be careful when using commentaries. That is, a commentary represents the fullness of scholarship *at a particular time* and the maturity of a method *at that time*. The phrase "at that time" emphasizes the fact that methods for studying the Bible, and the understandings that derive from them, continue to develop and evolve. What may have been the best we could do (as far as understanding goes) in the past may not be the best we can do (or say) in the present.

Biblical scholarship has advanced tremendously in the last fifty years. Other methods of interpretation have been refined. New archaeological and literary evidence has been discovered and analyzed. New methods of interpretation have been advanced, and old categories of distinction have been analyzed and reconfigured. For example, the age-old distinction between the New Testament and other early Christian literature is beginning to be dismantled, and scholars are starting to speak only of early Christian literature. Similarly, the study of early Christianity is becoming the study of early Christianities under the realization that Christianity was much more diverse than we originally thought. Older commentaries did not (and could not!) take into account the new insights available to modern biblical scholars. In short, in many ways, older volumes are out of date.

Commentaries must be used carefully. Certain commentaries, although old, still represent the most that scholarship can say about a particular text. Thus, in certain areas an older commentary may still be the one used most by scholars—and it will usually be called the "standard" work on the subject. For example, New Testament scholar Rudolf Bultmann's commentary on the Gospel of John is still widely considered the standard work on the subject. Of course, other good commentaries on John have been written, but the consensus in the scholarly community is that these other commentaries have not reached the same level of mature, thoughtful reflection as Bultmann's. Likewise, Gerhard von Rad's *Old Testament Theology* is still a must-read text for anyone seeking to do serious work in scholarship on the Hebrew Bible. In this case, scholars do not believe that von Rad's insights are still entirely correct, but von Rad's commentary sets out the framework within which all subsequent commentaries on the topic occur. So the fact that a commentary is old does not *necessarily* disqualify its use in modern biblical interpretation.

What is your responsibility as an astute reader of biblical scholarship? When using a commentary on the Bible, make sure that it takes into account the best current scholarship in the field. This can be difficult to ascertain. The best solution appears to be to read more than one commentary. Consult book reviews in biblical journals to see how scholars react to a new commentary. (There will, however, be a time lag between the publication of a commentary and the publication of book reviews on it.) You can also consult books that give an overview of scholarship on a particular subject, that seek to inform us about advances made in biblical research. This requires more work than just sticking with the first commentary you find, but the reward for your extra effort is the knowledge that you are reading the best scholarship on the subject.

RULE OF THUMB 23: Although articles are at the cutting edge of biblical scholarship, they are not always a scholar's most mature thoughts.

Articles are the lifeblood of scholarship and are important pieces in the overall scholarly dialogue. However, articles represent the beginning of a scholarly conversation more than the end result of analysis. And it is important to keep this in mind when you read them.

Articles represent scholars' attempts to question traditional scriptural interpretations or to expand our knowledge into areas previously unstudied. Because an article is often the beginning of a scholarly dialogue, when we read it, we should ask some fundamental questions regarding the article's thesis. For example, on what basis does the author call into question our prior understanding of the subject? Was some new document found? Has some archaeological discovery challenged our previous historical model? Does the author use some method of interpretation that shines new light on the possible meaning of the passage? Has the author found some logical flaw in the work of other scholars? Does the author take insights derived from one discipline, like literary analysis, and apply them in new and insightful ways to the study of the Bible? These are the kinds of questions that need to be answered.

Many scholarly journals publish the latest insights on the study of the Bible, the best known being the *Journal of Biblical Literature*, the quarterly publication of the Society of Biblical Literature. Outside of commentaries and other books, it is in these journals that we come into contact with the most thought-provoking ideas in biblical study. However, we are required as astute readers to pay close attention to the claims made in an article. We must also pay attention over time to the responses of other scholars to the article. Scholars write responses to an article, sometimes supporting its conclusions, sometimes disputing them. The initial article may also be used as a cornerstone for another article, using the same method or evidence the first author used. What is key is that the original article begins the dialogue and sparks the debate.

Since an article represents an attempt to extend our knowledge, we must be careful not to accept its ideas uncritically. Just as with commentaries—and all publications, in fact—we must weigh the credibility of the article against other available evidence. One of the easiest ways to do a cursory analysis of an article's credibility is to look at the footnotes. A maxim about scholarship that I believe to be true holds that *the real work of scholarship occurs in the footnotes*. While footnotes are no guarantee that the article is entirely credible, they do tell us a lot about the scholars and scholarship with which the author is in conversation. In the footnotes we can detect the real debates behind the article's claim(s).

An example of how articles develop into mature scholarly thought is the work on the Sermon on the Mount done by one of my professors, Hans Dieter Betz. In 1973 Professor Betz wrote an article entitled "A Jewish-Christian Cultic *Didache* in Matt. 6:1–18: Reflections and Questions on the Problem of the Historical Jesus." This article opened a conversation on the Sermon on the Mount that was not completed until the mid-1990s. Betz wrote six more articles on related topics. The scholarly conversation also continued in articles written by other scholars, and in conversations at conferences, in classrooms, and around water coolers. These conversations introduced scholars to Betz's ideas, and scholars, through their insight, helped Betz further refine his argument. In 1985 seven of these articles were published in the book *Essays on the Sermon on the Mount*. All the while, Betz and other scholars were working out and refining the implications of his ideas. Finally, Betz's most mature thoughts on the Sermon on the Mount appeared in his 1995 commentary *The Sermon on the Mount*, in the Hermeneia series. Each article had represented a step in the process that ultimately created the great commentary we have now.

The work of senior scholars forms the foundation for the further work of younger scholars. Younger scholars take the work of senior scholars in new directions. Professor Betz's ideas about the Sermon on the Mount had an impact on my own scholarship. As a graduate student in his course on the Lord's Prayer, I became interested in the role and purpose of instructions regarding the performance of rituals (what Betz calls "cultic *didache*") in the

New Testament and the early church. As a student in that course, I became intrigued as to why Clement of Alexandria does not discuss the Lord's Prayer in his own essay on prayer. This led me to write an essay entitled "Why Clement of Alexandria Would Not Pray the Lord's Prayer," which represented my first ideas on and my first attempt to talk about how people in the early church understood what prayer meant and was supposed to do. Later, through conversations with professors I decided that further investigation into this area would be useful. I chose Clement of Alexandria as one of my subjects of study and balanced his views against those of Tertullian of Carthage, and this became the basis of my dissertation. My scholarship owes a tremendous debt to that initial article written by Hans Dieter Betz.

This is how scholarship works. One idea grows out of and builds upon another. Each idea helps us to understand more and more about the Bible and the world from which it came. The process begins with the initial article and, if things go well, eventually culminates in a mature commentary (or commentaries) on a scriptural text. But if you compare that initial article to the scholar's most mature writing, you most likely find that the scholar's ideas have been refined or even changed in the process.

This is why this rule of thumb is so important. An article does not end debate on a topic; it begins it. The astute reader of biblical scholarship must keep this important fact in mind.

RULE OF THUMB 24: While a scholar may be correct on some matters, this does not mean that the scholar is correct on all matters.

Other than pointing out the obvious—that an individual is not always correct about all things at all times—this rule of thumb serves as a nudge to remind you that scholarship is not a one-sided dialogue conducted only by credentialed specialists. Biblical scholarship is larger than just what goes on in colleges and universities. It can occur wherever and whenever a person practices the discipline properly. Of course, a certain amount of knowledge is necessary, and the rules of the discipline always apply, but the student of biblical scholarship should not be lulled into the false mind-set that only scholars can read and interpret the Bible properly. As a student in a biblical studies course, you have the obligation to act the way a scholar does when you examine a text. This means that you must weigh the evidence for yourself.

The reason you are required, as a student, to act like a scholar in your study of the Bible is fundamental to this rule of thumb: *Scholars can be wrong in their examination of the evidence.* This does not mean that scholars are intentionally wrong, that is, when they *are* wrong. As I noted in my discussion about my dissertation, sometimes scholars simply do not see another way to answer the question(s) raised by their investigation. Why is this the case? They may have tunnel vision when it comes to their particular subject (see the discussion in Rule of Thumb 21). Or they may lack necessary evidence that would change their conclusion. For example, our understanding of first-century C.E. Galilee is changing due to the ongoing archaeological excavations at locations such as ancient Sepphoris. Commentaries, books, and articles written, say, ten years or so ago may be incorrect in some of their analyses of scriptural texts, particularly those that depend upon a correct understanding of the society of the time.

I remember being disturbed as a student when I read Rudolf Bultmann's *Primitive Christianity*. I had always thought highly of Bultmann's scholarship, but in *Primitive Christianity*, Bultmann's analysis of Judaism in the time of Jesus reflects a bias common prior to World War II. Although Bultmann does not come out and say that the

Jews worship God the wrong way, he makes it clear that he believes that Christianity is a vital and necessary improvement upon Judaism. He makes this sentiment clear by his corrosive use of the term "legalistic."

Bultmann identifies Pharisaic Judaism as the dominant form of Judaism in Jesus' time. (Pharisaic Judaism developed into rabbinic Judaism—the dominant form of Judaism today—after the destruction of the Temple in 70 C.E.) He then labels this form of Judaism "legalistic," by which he means that it falls short of the ideal of the true worship of God. In short, legalism means false worship. And this false worship, he argues, is the basis for modern Judaism, which means that the Judaism we know today is no better than the Judaism condemned by Jesus. Add to this troubling analysis the political and religious context of post–World War 1 Germany, and Bultmann's comments about first-century C.E. Judaism certainly appear very inflammatory.

The truth is that anti-Semitism was acceptable, even among scholars, prior to the Holocaust, and Bultmann's labeling of the Jews as "legalistic" demonstrates precisely how biased scholarship was.

What did I do? I questioned whether it was ethical for Bultmann to label the Jews as "legalistic" at a time when the forces of Nazism, which would lead to the Holocaust, were gathering in his country. I believed that he should have known better. On the other hand, I realized that my disapproval of Bultmann might be really unfair because I was attempting to judge Bultmann's actions on the basis of our contemporary values and knowledge. So I talked to a number of my professors about the book. They were divided. Some felt as I did—Bultmann should have known better. Others felt that it was unfair to judge Bultmann by modern American standards. I was confused, to say the least.

Since then, I have come to learn a number of things. First, anti-Semitism was more pervasive and acceptable in the 1930s and 1940s than we realize today. Bultmann's comments, which offended me, were actually a moderating of a more vicious view of Jews prevalent at that time. Second, Bultmann's understanding of Judaism in Jesus' time was based on information that is recognized today as incorrect. Pharisaism was *not* the predominant form of Judaism in the first century C.E. In fact, we now know that it would be at least two centuries *after* the destruction of the Temple before the rabbis actually began to exercise control over the synagogues. There was no dominant form of Judaism in Jesus' time, unless you count the age-old worship of God through sacrifice at the Temple as a dominant form of worship. Modern scholars now speak of ancient Judaisms rather than Judaism.

Third, and finally, although Bultmann cannot be held responsible for things he did not and could not know about Judaism in the time of Jesus, he can, however, be held responsible for the manner in which he used the information at his disposal. This means that Bultmann's understanding of ancient Judaism must now be pronounced as wrong, and, in fact, no serious scholar today would argue that Bultmann's depiction in *Primitive Christianity* should function as an entirely trustworthy account of what Jesus' world was like. Does this mean, however, that Bultmann's book has nothing important to tell us about early Christianity? No. Although Bultmann was wrong about the so-called legalistic character of first-century Judaism, he does offer some important insights that help us better understand early Christianity. Thus, our need for Rule of Thumb 24.

When reading scholarship we must be careful to look at the evidence carefully. Scholars do the best they can in analyzing the evidence at their disposal, but sometimes their analysis is wrong. Later evidence may prove the analysis to be wrong. Or a scholar may simply be unaware of available evidence that disproves his or her analysis.

Regardless of the reasons for a mistaken analysis, being wrong on some issues does not make one wrong on all issues. Likewise, being correct when it comes to most things does not mean that we are correct on everything. As an astute reader of biblical scholarship, you must exercise the same caution in reading a scholar's analysis of a biblical text that you would in reading the Bible itself (see Rule of Thumb 1). As we noted regarding Rule of Thumb 20, scholars have prejudices like everyone else, and these prejudices can color their understanding of certain biblical texts in a way that the weight of the evidence will prove to be wrong.

4

Rules of Thumb for Surviving Biblical Scholarship

RULE OF THUMB 25: Tradition is important, but it's not everything.

Tradition is so much a part of our lives that often we fail to recognize it when we see it. Tradition is what is passed down from one generation to the next. It can be something as simple as closing your eyes when you pray, which is as much a tradition as the practice in some churches of celebrating the Lord's Supper on the first Sunday of each month. Tradition is important because it gives us a sense of order and connectedness to those who have come before us. It would not be an overstatement to say that we could not be who we are without tradition.

All these great things about tradition aside, it does have a down side. The problem arises when tradition is kept for its own sake, that is, when it loses its meaning, when we continue to do things—or act in particular ways—out of habit and not because our behavior continues our connectedness to our forebears. As a pastor, I often experienced a problem when I wanted to change one of the time-honored customs of our church. The response to my request for change would be "Why? We've *always* done it that way." That is a hallmark of tradition, and hearing it warned me that I had to be careful about the manner in which I suggested changes, because people had done this activity this way for so long that they no longer remembered why they had decided to do it that way in the first place.

When a tradition ceases to be meaningful, however—meaningful tradition being synonymous with what Roman Catholics call "living tradition"—it has to be altered in some fashion. This is true of how we live out our faith in our religious communities, and of biblical scholarship.

One scholarly tradition that has been altered by biblical scholarship is the authorship of the Gospels. The common understanding of Gospel authorship is that men named Matthew, Mark, Luke, and John wrote the four Gospels. Most nonscholars believe that these four men were all disciples of Jesus. That is, they were actual witnesses to the events of Jesus' ministry, which guarantees the truthfulness of their testimony regarding Jesus. The majority of biblical scholars do not understand Gospel authorship quite in that way. The four Gospels themselves do not contain any real information regarding their authorship. That is, none of them says, "This was written by Matthew," or "This was written by Luke." In fact, we are not quite sure who wrote the four Gospels contained in the Bible. Scholars use the traditional names for the Gospels in their writing about them because that is the easiest way to refer to the texts. So when they say, "Matthew says," they mean, "The Gospel traditionally attributed to Matthew says," because we are not sure who wrote the Gospel that tradition has ascribed to Matthew. In this way scholars have altered the traditional understanding of Gospel authorship.

While what scholars have done regarding Gospel authorship may seem slight, in other areas, scholarship has raised questions that cannot be settled so easily. It is in these areas (for example, the dating of the exodus story) that most students of biblical scholarship experience the most difficulties. In my estimation, these difficulties arise primarily because tradition has been confused with an old Catholic definition of truth: "what has been believed always, everywhere, and by all." That is to say, we sometimes confuse tradition with absolute, unchangeable truth. When we realize that what we have taken to be absolutely true is really an aspect of tradition, we become frustrated and angry. This frustration or anger is often rooted in the sudden experience of a *lack* of connectedness to what has been. A friend of mine in seminary once said after a Bible class, "They're trying to take away my Jesus!" What she had always thought to be true about Jesus and the Bible had suddenly come under attack, and she had no idea how to respond.

So, what do you need? Survival skills.

Survival Skills

To complete a biblical studies course successfully, you need survival skills, skills that will make your study of the Bible an enjoyable experience, skills that will lessen the sense of loss my friend felt in her first Bible class. And I have three for you: (1) Remember that there is no such thing as absolute or unchangeable truth when it comes to interpreting the Bible; (2) remember that traditional authority is mediated authority; and (3) remember living tradition means changing tradition.

1. *There is no such thing as absolute or unchangeable truth when it comes to interpreting the Bible.* This first survival skill is really more of a working premise. As we discussed with Rules of Thumb 18 and 19, there is a difference between a fact and the interpretation (or conclusion) we draw from it. A fact is a "thing" or "datum of experience" that we possess. The meaning of the fact

depends on the person investigating it. For example, the life of Julius Caesar is a fact of Roman history. Whether or not Julius Caesar was a good or great person is an interpretation of that fact. A fact is as distinct from its interpretation as the Bible is from the interpretations we derive from it. That is, a fact and its interpretation are related, but they are also different. Facts, as data of experience, seldom change, while interpretations, which are attempts to make sense of facts, are expected to change when the necessity arises.

This also applies to tradition and traditional biblical interpretations. Let me suggest one way you can understand the concept of truth. For me, what makes an interpretation "good" or "right" or "true" is that it takes into account all the relevant facts in a way that makes sense. As long as an interpretation makes sense in light of what I know about the facts under discussion, it can be called truthful. On the other hand, when an interpretation fails to make sense, it can no longer be deemed truthful. But what does it mean to say that something is true?

The words "true" and "truth" come from older English words meaning "faithful" or carrying a sense of faithfulness to something, so that what is true is what is faithful to what has gone before. The Greek word for truth carries with it a similar understanding. In Greek, what is true is what is worth remembering (literally, what is not forgotten). Therefore, when we say that an interpretation is true, we mean that it has proven itself faithful to the facts and is worth remembering. Tradition is what is passed down from one group to another because it is worth remembering. It is somehow faithful to the original experience from which it comes.

Therefore, we can say that tradition is the truth when it is faithful to the facts and worth passing on to others. Built into the natures of tradition and truth is the idea that we must reexamine the facts periodically, especially when new data come to light. As we accumulate more facts and try to understand them, we may discover that our traditional interpretations no longer make sense in light of the evidence. In that case, our interpretations are no longer true and are thus unworthy of our allegiance. The aim of biblical scholars is not to destroy tradition or truth, but rather to make sure that what is passed down is worthy of remembering. In short, absolute (by which I mean unchangeable) interpretations cannot exist in a discipline in which we are constantly uncovering new facts. The Bible as a fact may be absolute, but our interpretations of it are in constant need of revision.

2. *Traditional authority is mediated authority*. Understanding this will help you survive biblical scholarship. In this case, the authority begins with the original religious experiences of ancient people with God. Those experiences were then written in a collection of works that some people understood to represent their faith. Next, the church, through a series of councils, adopted a number of these writings as representative of its faith, and called this collection the Bible. Finally, people in church now read and understand the Bible as representative of their faith.

Again, an analysis of our terms is important. "Authority" comes from the Latin *auctoritas,* meaning a permanent quality that enables an idea or thing to exercise lasting and decisive influence over others. To "mediate" means to occupy a middle position or to be the mechanism or instrument by which something is passed on. Mediated authority is, therefore, authority that comes to us by means of something else. In the case of biblical study, we must make a distinction between the authority of the Bible and the authority of biblical interpretations.

The Bible has authority because it mediates between us and God. That is, the Bible has authority to the degree that it is the instrument by which we come to understand the authority of God. In reality, the authority does not belong to the Bible but to God. Or to say it another way, the Bible would have no authority for us if it did not serve as the instrument by which we come to experience God. This authority is traditional to the extent that people before us experienced this reality and deemed the Bible worth passing down to us. When scholars attempt to understand the Bible, they are not trying to undermine its authority as a collection of documents worthy of being passed down. On the contrary, by studying the Bible with such great care, they uphold the idea that the Bible has authority. Yet they recognize that the Bible's authority is not the same as God's. God's authority is absolute, while the Bible's authority is derived from the authority of God.

We must similarly distinguish between the Bible's authority and the authority of biblical interpretation. The authority of the Bible is derived from the authority of God, and, in turn, the authority of biblical interpretation is derived from the authority of the Bible. Biblical authority is a mediated authority because it depends on the mechanism of the biblical interpreter, who helps us understand what the Bible is saying, who mediates between us and the Bible.

The apostle Paul alludes to this type of authority when he asks, "And how are they to hear without someone to proclaim him? And how are they to proclaim him unless they are sent?" (Rom. 10:14c–15a). People before us have found certain interpretations of the Bible to be helpful in the quest for understanding. This is what we mean by *traditional interpretations*. These interpretations are truthful to the extent that they are faithful to the facts. However, when the facts change, we (both scholars and nonscholars) are required to change our interpretations to remain faithful to the facts. In other words, the authority of an interpretation is only as good as the ability of the interpreter to make sense of the facts as derived from the Bible and elsewhere. So questioning the authority of an interpretation is not the same as questioning the authority of the Bible itself. Nor is questioning the authority of an interpretation the same as questioning the authority of God.

3. *Living tradition means changing tradition.* Recognizing this will help us survive an encounter with biblical scholarship. Tradition is what is passed down as worthy of remembrance. Being worthy of remembrance implies a faithfulness to the original event itself. This is the idea behind the Christian sacrament of the Lord's Supper, or Eucharist. When Christians partake in the tradition of the Eucharist, they re-create the original event of Jesus' last meal with his disciples. Paul mentions this in his discussion of the Eucharist: "I commend you because you remember me in everything and maintain the traditions just as I handed them on to you" (1 Cor. 11:1).

At the same time, however, the tradition of the Eucharist has changed over two millennia. When the earliest Christians began celebrating the Eucharist, they actually had a meal (cf. 1 Cor. 11:17–26). This was not a problem, because the early churches were actually individuals' homes. As the churches grew and Christianity became a legal religion, however, meetings were moved out of houses and into buildings called basilicas. This change in location meant that the tradition of the Eucharist meal changed from a full-blown meal to the two basic elements of the meal, bread and wine. Much later, because of some Protestant concerns about alcohol, in some observances grape juice replaced the wine. In form, the tradition has changed considerably. It is no longer the same meal that Jesus shared with his closest followers. As a meaningful remembrance of Jesus' last meal, however, the Eucharist still re-creates that event.

On the other hand, when a tradition is meaningful to its current practitioners, its form may be retained. For example, in the African Methodist Episcopal Church, my own branch of Methodism, we still kneel at the chancel rail during the Lord's Supper, a practice that goes back to pre-Reformation Roman Catholicism. Catholics used to kneel at the altar in order to receive communion from the priest, and when the Church of England separated from the Roman Catholic Church under the leadership of King Henry VIII, the Church of England kept this practice. Methodism began as a movement within the Church of England. Its founder, John Wesley, retained the practice in the liturgy he sent with the first Methodist bishops to the United States. Richard Allen, the founder of the African Methodist Episcopal Church, further retained the practice in the first liturgy of the A.M.E. Church. It has been part of African Methodist tradition ever since.

Today, Catholics no longer kneel when taking the Lord's Supper. The Church of England retains the practice, but its American counterpart, the Protestant Episcopal Church, does not. The United Methodist Church, the heir of the original Methodist Episcopal Church, no longer requires that persons kneel at communion. Yet the A.M.E. Church still finds the tradition meaningful. I believe that part of the reason African Methodists retain the practice has to do with the founding of the denomination itself, which according to A.M.E. tradition, occurred as a result of an incident that took place while people were kneeling at the chancel rail: Richard Allen left St. George Methodist Church in protest because he was forcibly dragged from his knees during worship. So when African Methodists kneel at the chancel rail during communion, they not only re-create the last supper of Jesus, they also re-create the event that founded the church itself. In this case what is passed down is retained because it is meaningful. However, this does not mean that the tradition should be continued just because it is a tradition. It is retained because it is meaningful, but if such a tradition were to lose its meaning, it would be necessary to change it.

In sum, we must develop certain skills or techniques in order to survive successfully our encounter with biblical scholarship. First, we must remember that biblical interpretations are not timelessly true. Rather, they are reasonably adequate understandings of the scriptural text based on the information available. Second, we must remember that questioning a traditional interpretation of the Bible is not the same as questioning God's authority. And, finally, we must remember that for a traditional interpretation to be retained in the tradition, it must be meaningful or worth remembering.

RULE OF THUMB 26: When it comes to asking questions, God is a "big boy," God can handle it.

The writer of 2 Timothy tells his reader, "Do your best to present yourself to God as one approved by him, a worker who has no need to be ashamed, rightly explaining the word of truth" (2:15). (Some students remember the KJV rendering of the last phrase, "rightly dividing the word of truth.") The writer of Hebrews tells his reader that an infant in the faith is one "unskilled in the word of righteousness" (5:13) and the mature person in the faith is one "whose faculties have been trained by practice to distinguish good from evil" (5:14). What these writers have in common is their shared belief that God expects us to be skilled in our use of the Bible—to *rightly* divide the word of truth. This means that your intellectual faculties—your ability to think and reason—must be trained. In short, there is an expectation in the Bible that persons of faith will exercise their mental abilities in order to make sense of scripture.

Some people believe that blind obedience is preferable to reasoned faith. I am not sure why. They seem to believe that questioning the Bible means questioning God. They believe that God is in some way offended by questions. Nothing could be further from the truth. In fact, life and faith demand that we ask certain essential questions. As the theologian Schubert Ogden has said, "To be human is not only to live, but also to understand one's life and, within limits, to be free to lead it and responsible for doing so. . . . This means that one's very life as a human being involves asking certain questions."[11] Questioning is part of faith. In fact, another theologian, Anselm, once defined life as *fides quaerens intellectum* ("faith seeking understanding").

Understanding is the goal of faith. However, among some modern people, the concept of faith has lost its genuine meaning. Nowadays, faith is defined by some as "belief in something unbelievable." Reason is seen as unreasonable, and some people are afraid that too much thinking will make you lose your faith. This does not make sense. One of the fundamental beliefs of Judaism and Christianity is that God made human beings as rational creatures. In fact, the ability to self-reflect is what makes human beings fundamentally different from other animals. It does not make sense that God would endow human beings with reason and then expect them not to use it when it comes to understanding life and faith. Hear what the apostle Paul says regarding Christian discipleship: "I appeal to you therefore, brothers and sisters, by the mercies of God, to present your bodies as a living sacrifice, holy and acceptable to God, which is your *reasonable form of divine service*. Do not be conformed to this world, but be transformed by the renewing of your minds, so that you may discern what is the will of God—what is good and acceptable and perfect" (Rom. 12:1–2, NRSV, my alteration in italics).

Notice the way the apostle phrases his appeal. He calls Christian discipleship a "reasonable form of divine service." The word used here in Greek is the one from which we get the word "logical." Paul is saying here that what is reasonable is also what is spiritual. This is confirmed by what he says next. He does not say that people are to renew their spirits or their souls but their *minds*. Why? So that they may *discern* the will of God. Paul is not just throwing these terms together. He means it. In his mind, the religious movement that will become Christianity is defined primarily by a certain intellectual quality. In short, Christianity, according to Paul, is a thinking person's religion.

Don't be afraid to ask questions in your exploration of the Bible. The goal of questioning is not to undermine God (or God's authority), but to *understand* God. However, understanding God is not an entirely objective matter. We come to the Bible with certain questions we want answered, and this gives understanding God a subjective component.

Asking questions says more about us as human beings than it does about God. When we ask questions of the Bible, we are not doing any real damage to the authority of God; rather, we are trying to understand ourselves and our relationship to God. God, being God, cannot be brought down by the questioning of human beings. God is certainly much bigger than that.

RULE OF THUMB 27: If your faith can't stand a little shaking, perhaps there wasn't much of a foundation there in the first place.

Jesus says in the Sermon on the Mount:

"Everyone then who hears these words of mine and acts on them will be like a wise man who built his house on rock. The rain fell, the floods came, and the winds blew and beat on that house, but it did not fall, because it had been founded on rock. And everyone who hears these words of mine and does not act on them will be like a foolish man who built his house on sand. The rain fell, and the floods came, and the winds blew and beat against that house, and it fell—and great was its fall!" (Matt. 7:24–27)

This statement by Jesus is addressed primarily to would-be disciples. I will not focus here on the exact meaning of the statement but will use the metaphors of the house built on rock and the house built on sand as a way of talking about biblical study and faith.

Many students come to biblical studies thinking that the faith they have prior to entering the halls of academia is a solid and unquestionable faith. In actuality, it is most likely an unchallenged faith. I asked a class one day, "How many of you read your Bibles on a regular basis?" Not one hand went up. I was amazed. All the students had professed to be people of faith, yet none of the students read their Bibles regularly. Moreover, although these students confessed to not reading their Bibles, they were sure that their faiths were biblically grounded. Furthermore, whenever questions arose in class that demanded some knowledge of the Bible, they could not point to the relevant texts, but they were nonetheless certain that the Bible supported their position.

An unchallenged faith is no better than building your house on sand. If you are not certain about what you believe, then can you say that you believe anything worthwhile at all? This is the real question that confronts the person of unchallenged faith. That is why I think it is important for students to read not only the Bible but also anti-Christian literature from the ancient world. And those anti-Christian writings notwithstanding, for many people, reading the Bible for the first time in an academic environment is a faith-challenging experience. This is where the "rubber meets the road" when it comes to understanding the depth and meaning of your faith, for many people find that faith is much more complicated than they first thought. What they understood as simple (that is, faith) has now become a matter of analysis: analyzing texts, analyzing traditions, and analyzing traditional interpretations.

I believe that it should be this way, especially for those who desire to lead faith communities. Leadership in these communities should be in the hands of those who know what they believe, people who have confronted and thought through their own issues of faith. When the storm that Jesus describes in the Sermon on the Mount does come, isn't it better to face it knowing what you believe and why you believe it? I see this as the pastoral role teachers can play in the lives of their students. We are there to challenge what students believe. The goal is twofold: to empower and to disempower at the same time.

Empowerment as a goal means helping students know exactly what the Bible says. Too many students *think* they know what the Bible says but don't actually know how to interpret its information. As I have noted throughout this book, reading the Bible involves more than just reading the Bible. Words mean nothing unless they are put together in a way that makes sense. Verses from the Bible mean nothing unless we can understand who they came from and why they were written. Knowing what the Bible means, rightly dividing the word of truth, was a liberating and empowering experience for me. I firmly believe that it can be the same for students, but for this to happen, students must first be disempowered in their study of the Bible.

To feel empowered by the study of the Bible, students need to know just how much about the Bible they don't know. It is only through disempowerment that one can become empowered. In some ways this is very different from other types of education. For example, in teaching the study of political science, you rarely come across persons who believe that they know what political science is. Students generally understand that when they walk into the political science classroom, they are going to study a subject about which they know very little. The same is true for many other academic disciplines. However, when it comes to religion, part of the process of learning means unlearning those things that are either misguided or wrong, according to the rules laid down by academics for the study of the Bible.

The benefit of having a challenged faith is that you are forced to do some significant soul-searching when it comes to what you think you believe. A challenged faith, which includes empowerment and disempowerment, is the foundation of rock described in the Sermon on the Mount. When you are forced to look at your faith seriously, you begin to know who you really are. In more academic terms, challenges to your faith help you form identity. Identity is that core understanding you have of who you are—what you believe and why. When it comes to being a full member of the human race, nothing is more important than the formation of identity. Whether you are a religious leader or a member of a religious community, you have a responsibility to yourself to determine the contours of your identity. You have a responsibility to find out if your faith is built upon rock or sand.

RULE OF THUMB 28: Faith is not like dominoes. When one part falls, it doesn't mean that all of it will fall.

There used to be a theory in American foreign policy called the domino theory. In a nutshell, the policy maintained that other countries in other regions would topple like dominoes if the United States allowed one country to fall to communism. If you have ever seen dominoes lined up and tipped, the argument may be very compelling. However, one thing many people overlooked in this analogy is that countries are not dominoes. There are all kinds of reasons that particular countries develop their political systems, and reducing this complex matter to the level of dominoes demonstrates how little we actually understood about such things.

In a similar fashion, some have said that faith is like a series of lined-up dominoes. The consequence in this analogy is the same as it is in the political analogy: if you allow someone to change your mind about one tenet of faith—one domino in the lineup—your other tenets will fall along with it.

As you will probably guess from the wording of this rule of thumb, I do not believe this to be true *in an unqualified sense.* I use the phrase "unqualified sense" purposely, because, although I do not buy the "domino theory of faith," I do think that our ideas about religion form faith systems similar to other organic systems. I will attempt to develop this idea a little later, but let me first concentrate on why the "domino theory of faith" is misguided.

The first problem is that the domino theory sees faith as belief in certain propositional truths. That is, this view sees faith as a body of doctrine that the believer must hold to be true, what theologians call *fides quae creditur* (the faith that is believed). This type of faith is not necessarily wrong in itself, but it can become misguided when it is joined to a fundamentalist notion of the inspiration and infallibility of the Bible. When this occurs, faith becomes the belief that the Bible in its entirety must either be accepted as true or rejected as false. In other words, if the Bible says that the world was created in seven days, it must have been created in seven days. Otherwise, the Bible is proven to be false, and faith has no basis in truth.

Let me give you an example. A man I knew believed that he needed to accept so-called "creation biology" because the Bible gave him an anchor in life. He believed that if God "lied" to him in part of the Bible, God could not be trusted to tell the truth in other parts. This defense implies that reading the Bible is somehow fully equivalent to having a conversation with God. It implies that this man has no knowledge of life that would allow him to discriminate between degrees of truth or levels of meaning in the Bible.

It also implies that every mistake in the Bible means some-one is lying—in this case, God. At the same time, this naive man claims to be able to know beyond a doubt that one book is *the* book, and all of it must be absolutely true, or else it is of no religious help at all.

Of course the Bible is not the only book for which similar religious claims are made. In Islam it is the Qur'an. In Hinduism it is the Bhagavad Gita. For Judaism the text Christians identify as the Old Testament is the entire Bible. This man disagrees with countless other religious people, including millions of Christians who do not hold his view of the Bible. This man claims he has no knowledge of anything that would enable him to see more truth in some parts of the Bible than in others. How then, can he possibly form a reasonable judgment as to whether the Bible—or any book for that matter—could be the infallible God addressing us in human words in such a way that we cannot be mistaken as to its meaning? This is really the idea we are dealing with here.

Fundamentally, the question of what the Bible says hinges on how one views the idea of revelation. To people like this man, there are just two, opposite ways and only these two ways to understand revelation: (1) there is an absolutely infallible—yet humanly accessible—special source of knowledge in religion, or (2) there is no source whatsoever of knowledge deserving any trust or confidence. This view is strange to me because we do not require this kind of absolute knowledge in any other area of life. For example, scientists do not claim any result of science as absolutely certain as it stands, yet our engineers apply many scientific results with confidence. And even if it were true that there are no absolutely infallible sources of religious knowledge, this would not mean that just any person walking down the street is as likely to be of help in religious matters as were the saints or religious founders of history. Nor would it mean that any other book is as likely to contain religious wisdom as the Bible or other sacred writings. The choice is not between absolutely certain and reliable revelation on the one hand and no revelation on the other. There can be many degrees in between. The same is true of biblical interpretation.

As I said earlier, the primary purpose of biblical study has been historical, that is, to answer the question, "What has the Christian witness of faith *already been* in the lives of human beings?" In this, biblical study is part of the overall work of writing and understanding history, and it is governed by the same rules. On the other hand, the Bible has always held a special place in Christianity. In fact, Christians refer to it as the "canon," which means the norm of Christian teaching and practice. However, when we hear that word, we do not always understand what it really means.

The Protestant Reformers referred to the Bible as "the norm that norms but is not normed [in the process]" (*norma, sed non normata*). What this means is that there is a "center" or "norm" to Christian theology that is contained in, *but is not identical with*, the Bible. According to Christians, this center is Jesus Christ, or at least the tradition of the apostles regarding Christ. As I said earlier in Rule of Thumb 25, there is something that gives the Bible its authority, and for Christians this is Christ. In essence, scripture is subject to the authority of Jesus Christ. A corollary statement can be made for Judaism's use of the Hebrew Bible (e.g., for Judaism the center of Jewish theology is God, and it is God who gives scripture its authority).

The canon is a collection of writings produced by the early church and gradually recognized by it as the primary authority for its faith, witness, and theology. In this sense, the canon is the embodiment of a history of decisions on the part of the church. In other words, the New Testament is a product of the experience of the church. It was the way the church attempted to direct and guide people in their understanding of Jesus Christ. But since, as the Protestant Reformers said, "popes and councils can err," the canon that has been passed down to us from the early church is and must be open to revision. (The only authorities not open to revision in this process are Christ or God.) Thus, the canon is not a collection of writings recognized as authoritative by the early church. Rather, the canon is whatever it is in those writings that is authorized by Christ through the church's continuing experience under the guidance of the Holy Spirit. In the end the Bible is not a collection of propositional truths. The domino theory is wrong.

What did we learn from this discussion? In reading the Bible in an academic environment, expect that your ideas will be challenged and that some will change. Changing our ideas is a necessary part of the overall process of learning. However, changing ideas is not the same as abandoning ideas. Many people believe that the Bible ought to be the primary authority for a person's faith and witness in the world. To a certain degree this makes sense, but there is a necessary limit to this authority. If you believe that the Bible is the only place from which you can develop theology, then the Bible becomes the only proof necessary for the truth of that theology. This is a circular argument, no better than a parent telling a child to do something "because I say so." You did not buy that reasoning when you were a child; why should you buy it now?

The Bible's authority is a secondary authority. Therefore, merely to establish that an idea, practice, or assertion comes from the Bible or is supported by the Bible is not enough to authorize it as appropriate for people of faith. The Bible may say it, but that does not mean that we have to do it. Otherwise, we would still be practicing human slavery. There must be something more. In order for an idea or practice found in the Bible to be worthy of our following today, it must agree with the witness of Jesus as passed on to us by the apostles and the continuing guidance of the Holy Spirit.

In the end, we must recognize that our faith is similar to, yet different from, the faith of those who have come before us. The best model for understanding this is one used by the apostle Paul—the body of Christ. Christian faith is like a living organism. In a corporate sense, what we know as Christianity is the result of a process of growth from infancy (the early church) to adulthood (the modern church). As adults we are a compendium of all the experiences we have had. Some things we used to do we still do. Some we do not. Some ideas we used to believe we still believe. Others we do not. Yet all of these things—what has been kept and what has been laid aside—are a part of who we are today. Furthermore, we are still changing. We do not have the same challenges today that we had in our younger days, but neither do we face the same ailments or limitations.

As this is true of Christianity in a corporate sense, it is true of each one of us as human beings. Our faith—both as the church and as human beings—is a living faith. It will change as it confronts new times, new circumstances, and new information. That faith changes, but it does not cease to be faith. Faith is not like dominoes. It is something far more dynamic and powerful.

5

Concluding Remarks

This book has been as much a sharing of my experience as it has been an introduction to the discipline of biblical studies. It is not an easy discipline in which to engage. In part, the problem surrounding biblical studies is that it involves something we hold to be very meaningful in our lives—our religion. And whenever we talk about something so pivotal and personal, we run the risk of upsetting some and discouraging others. However, precisely because our religion is so meaningful, it is important for us to discuss it in a disciplined and somewhat detached manner, and this is what biblical studies seeks to do.

I took my initial Bible class because I thought it would be an easy grade. I had grown up in the church, a member of a ministerial family. I went to Sunday school and participated in our church's youth group, and I figured that this background had prepared me quite well for a college course in Bible. Boy, was I wrong! Not only that, the class had more than a hundred students in it, and over half of them failed the course. We were all wrong in our expectations. Yet the challenge of biblical studies invigorated me in a way that no other subject ever did. In just a short time I began to integrate biblical studies with classical studies, and the insights on the ancient world that I received helped to bring the biblical world to life. I fell in love. To be honest, I am still in love with biblical studies and antiquity. The ancient world was quite unlike our modern world. On the one hand, people in antiquity mingled in a way that we cannot duplicate with our modern concerns for race, class, and nationality. On the other hand, people in the ancient world could be quite vicious and intolerant when it came to issues of ethnicity and power. This is reflected in the Bible both explicitly and implicitly. I see it as my calling in life to carry this message about our common humanity into the classroom and use it as a tool to affect the lives of my students, and thereby the world. Teachers have an immense responsibility for shaping the future course of civilization. We are the ones who have the greatest effect upon the thinking of future generations. One recent study noted that when college days are past, students do not remember who was college president. They do not remember the support staff at the institution. What they remember are those teachers who challenged them to think in ways they had never imagined. They remember those teachers who gave them a glimpse into the full meaning of our common humanity.

Unfortunately, the Bible or antiquity by itself does not communicate this meaningfulness of humanity. Rather, it is the teacher who is able to "translate" the artifacts of Bible and history into the modern world in a way that makes that glimpse meaningful. I think this was what the apostle Paul hinted at when he said, "But how are they to call on one in whom they have not believed? And how are they to believe in one of whom they have never heard? And how are they to hear without someone to proclaim him? And how are they to proclaim him unless they are sent? . . . So faith comes from what is heard, and what is heard comes through the word of Christ" (Rom. 10:14–15a, 17). In this passage Paul is talking about spreading the gospel, but I think the same principle is at work in teaching. That is, people will never, and can never, know how meaningful the academic study of religion is unless there is someone to proclaim it. Proclamation is central to what it means to be Christian, and it is central to what it means to be a teacher. In truth, life-changing experiences come by means of coming into contact with a meaningful message. Teaching is serious business.

Thomas Aquinas once said, "Theology is a way of life" (*Theologia habitus est*). I believe this statement to be invariably true. The study of religion, theology in its most basic form, has the ability to change your life. Biblical studies, a part of what theologians call historical theology, plays a major part in changing people's lives. I have had the fortunate opportunity to see this happen again and again in my classrooms. Students who thought religion was one of those things to talk about, but not to engage intimately, had their minds completely changed. I have seen mathematics and chemistry majors change to religion, and I know many more who doubled majored (with one of those majors being religion) in order to allow this most interesting of subjects to change the way they speak, act, and think in the world. Seeing these changes continues to be an amazing experience for me. For me, theology really is a way of life. Furthermore, theology has become a way of life for countless students in a multitude of courses in classrooms across the country and the world.

The primary means by which biblical studies changes people's lives is its distinctive opportunity to allow modern persons to peer into the lives of religious people in the past. When we read the Bible, we not only encounter incredible depth of emotion and religious insight, but we also get the opportunity to reflect on what it meant to be a person living thousands of years ago; and we begin to realize that what it means to be human has not changed much over the millennia. People in antiquity struggled with some of the same issues that we do today. The patriarch Joseph had problems in his relationship with his siblings.

The struggle between them was so intense that his brothers sold him into slavery into Egypt. Later he was jailed because of the false accusation of a scorned would-be lover. However, these tragic experiences did not destroy his ability to realize his full potential as a human being. He rose, because of his special gifts, from the ignominy of a prison cell to the second highest governmental position of the time. And what is most surprising about this biblical story is that it rarely mentions the name of God, and God is not a major actor in the story. This story is so compelling because it resonates with many of our own experiences. Joseph struggled with some of our issues, and yet he prevailed. Later, the apostle Paul would echo these kinds of sentiments when he wrote, "But we have this treasure in clay jars, so that it may be made clear that this extraordinary power belongs to God and does not come from us. We are afflicted in every way, but not crushed; perplexed, but not driven to despair; persecuted, but not forsaken; struck down, but not destroyed; always carrying in the body the death of Jesus, so that the life of Jesus may also be made visible in our bodies" (2 Cor. 4:7–10). Many of us have gone through times of trial. We have felt afflicted, struck down, persecuted, and in despair. It is comforting not only to know that others have gone through similar circumstances, but also to know that they overcame them with the help of God. The Bible serves not only as the source of doctrine but as a rich resource of experiences for people of faith. These experiences help us understand what it means to be a human being in a world that does not always live up to our expectations.

Understanding the past for its own sake is not always very useful. When I was in school and studying people in the ancient world, I used to ask myself the question, So what? Many of us ask the same question when we read about people in the past, and we definitely confront the question when we enter an academic course on the Bible.

The question of relevance is the most pressing one for people reading the Bible. In our communities of faith, the minister gives us the answer. In the classroom, it is the responsibility of the instructor to assist you in making the connection between the past and the present. Any instructor who cannot assist us in that endeavor is not helping us to get the full range of meaning possible from our study— the design of the course notwithstanding.

As a resource for helping us understand our common humanity, the Bible opens up for us new worlds of understanding and possibility, worlds with the potential to change our lives. Yet this potential is activated only when we understand what the Bible is trying to tell us, and this means understanding it in its proper context. I am so dedicated to this idea that I always make a little wager with my students at the beginning of my introductory courses in Bible. I tell them that if they get through the whole semester and cannot say that they read something, or experienced something, or understood something that gave them a new glimpse into what it means to be a real human being, then I will give them an A for the course, no questions asked. Only one person ever told me that this Bible course did not change his life. Of course, that puts a lot of responsibility on me as the instructor, but I gladly accept this task. I *really* believe that what has changed my life has the capacity to change the lives of others. And when you really think about it, is that not what the gospel is all about?

In the end, I hope this book helps you navigate your way through the waters of biblical study. Understanding the Bible in an academic sense *can* make a difference in the way we live our lives. If this book assists you at all in understanding what goes on in your classroom, then it was well worth the effort. Biblical study is a powerful discipline that has the ability to transform our lives in ways that we never imagined, and as a student of biblical studies you have the potential for learning more about yourself and others than you ever dreamed.

   Theologia habitus est!

Notes

1. Modern versions of the KJV read, "And he spake to his sons, saying, Saddle me the ass. And they saddled *him.*"

2. Peter J. Gomes, *The Good Book: Reading the Bible with Mind and Heart* (New York: William Morrow and Co., 1996), 25.

3. Daniel Patte, *What Is Structural Exegesis?* Guides to Biblical Scholarship Series, ed. Dan O. Via Jr. (Philadelphia: Fortress Press, 1976), 83.

4. Gotthold Lessing, "On the Proof of the Spirit and of Power," in *Lessing's Theological Writings: Selections in Translation with an Introductory Essay,* ed. Henry Chadwick (Stanford, Calif.: Stanford University Press, 1957), 52 (emphasis mine).

5. Ibid., 54.

6. Ibid., 53.

7. Stephen Toulmin, *The Uses of Argument* (Cambridge: Cambridge University Press, 1958), 216.

8. Krister Stendahl, *Paul among Jews and Gentiles and Other Essays* (Philadelphia: Fortress Press, 1976), 35.

9. Title of an essay by Schubert Ogden. The essay can be found in *The Reality of God and Other Essays* (Dallas: Southern Methodist University Press, 1977), 120–43.

10. Michael Joseph Brown, "*Panem Nostrum:* The Problem of Petition and the Lord's Prayer," *Journal of Religion* (Oct. 2000).

11. Schubert Ogden, *Doing Theology Today* (Valley Forge, Pa.: Trinity Press, 1996), 22.